Richard L Miller

Travels Abroad

Holland, England, Belgium, France, Sandwich Islands, New Zealand, Australia,

Richard L Miller

Travels Abroad

Holland, England, Belgium, France, Sandwich Islands, New Zealand, Australia,

ISBN/EAN: 9783744727242

Printed in Europe, USA, Canada, Australia, Japan

Cover: Foto ©Andreas Hilbeck / pixelio.de

More available books at **www.hansebooks.com**

TRAVELS ABROAD:

EMBRACING

HOLLAND, ENGLAND, BELGIUM, FRANCE, SANDWICH ISLANDS, NEW ZEALAND, AUSTRALIA, &c.,

WITH

SOME REFLECTIONS ON THE PACIFIC COAST.

BY
RICHARD L. MILLER.

LYNCHBURG, VA.:
J. P. BELL COMPANY, STATIONERS AND PRINTERS.
1891.

To My Mother,

Who, above and beyond all others this side of the Better Country,

this modest volume is dedicated

By Her Son.

INTRODUCTION.

THE accompanying letters were written in the haste incident to travel, and were suggested by the dear ones at home, and by such friends as few men may claim; and for their own sakes, and as a tribute to them, this modest volume is submitted. There has rarely been an occasion in which a newspaper correspondent should be impelled to utter his thoughts in book form. This is not done in this instance with a view of immortality as a book-maker, but to gratify the dear ones in the home circle and the personal friends heretofore alluded to.

The writer has endeavored to portray things as they appeared to him. In the kaleidoscopic views it may be that the guide-books have been intrenched upon, but I trust the substance of the book will be recognized as my own.

The subjoined letters are published in this form, and addressed to my elder boy, Kenneth, for reasons that will be understood by every father.

R. L. MILLER.

Lynchburg, September, 1891.

SOUVENIRS OF TRAVEL.

LETTER I.

"SEEING THE ELEPHANT" AND VIEWING THE SUSPENSION BRIDGE IN NEW YORK—ON BOARD THE ETRURIA—A SQUALL AND ITS RESULTS—SHORTEST TIME ON RECORD—ARRIVAL IN LIVERPOOL.

LIVERPOOL, Sept. 7th, 1885.

KENNETH G. MILLER:

My Dear Boy—Soon after the arrival of our party in New York, we paid a visit to the famous suspension bridge connecting that city with Brooklyn. Its immensity can only be understood when you stand upon its highest point and take in a full view of New York, Brooklyn, and a river covered with vessels of every imaginable character, representing almost every civilized nation of the world, and where your view is limited only by the capacity of human vision. We spent two hours very pleasantly in Central Park and in the Art Gallery, notwithstanding our innate modesty received something of a shock at the nudity of the statues and the lack of drapery on the most popular paintings—rendered more conspicuous, indeed, by their absence. On the following day we "took in" the big elephant. I but state a positive fact when I say this "beast" is one hundred and seventy feet high, two hundred feet in length, and fifty feet wide. The "Houda" he carries on his back is about twenty by forty feet, and perhaps twenty feet high. For ten cents we gained admittance to the inside of the Mastodon, and as we stepped into the enclosure our eyes were confronted with a placard : " Enter by the leg only." It proved to be the left behind leg. It at once occurred to me what a treasure this leg would be to some friends at home as a " luck piece " to be carried around in the pocket with toes up. After climbing flight after flight of steps, we reached a large room about fifty feet square, known as the ballroom ; we then passed into numerous rooms, each capable of accommodating a dozen people comfortably, in the hollow of each of the Mastodon's cheeks. I have forgotten the number of the millions of feet of lumber and hundreds of squares of tin that were used in its construction. One of its feet—were it capable of locomotion—would cover nearly one-tenth of the three unpaved squares on " Fifth Avenue " in Lynchburg. How General S., C. & F. and the Messrs. K. would have enjoyed the aquarium building. Almost every species of sea-fish that could be seen in aquariums about two by four feet, supplied with fresh sea water through pipes which sent small streams bubbling through each of these receptacles.

Embarking on that floating palace, the Cunard steamship Etruria, on the 29th, we realized as she slowly floated seaward that we were indeed off for the "old countree." Promptly at 11 A. M. services were held in the dining saloon. Never before did I so greatly appreciate the beautiful hymn for the preservation of those "who go down to the sea in ships" as I did to day. As the sweet tones of the organ filled the immense saloon and the low-toned, devout voices joined in this petition to God, I could feel the throbbing of the engine, the rolling of the ship, and hear the continual "swish" of the water as it glided rapidly by. Then, and only then, did I fully realize what a dependent creature man is, how infinitesimally small he can at such times feel himself to be. Notwithstanding this is the sultry month of August at home, we are having an admirable illustration of December weather here. I am half frozen; the passengers on deck are wrapped in heavy overcoats, and wear a blue, pinched look, while those in the smoking room are steaming up with hot drinks. We made yesterday 472 nautical miles from 12 to 12 A. M., at which hour the distance is reckoned. To-day's log (31st) says 430 knots—equal to 508 land miles. Major S. P. H. has had the good fortune to see two whales and a school of porpoises—a privilege denied his companions. Up to the 2d of September I had seen no case of sea-sickness, but felt the time for that would inevitably come, and when old ocean begins to stir herself there would be a "casting up of accounts." Our vessel is almost a Great Eastern in its dimensions, and would require a more than ordinarily heavy sea to materially interfere with her progress.

At 2:30 P. M. a large sail vessel loomed up on our larboard, and although we are going in the same direction, the Etruria soon left her behind.

On the 2d we came through a booming gale; the waves were about the size of Friends' warehouse, and the hollows between as deep as the foundation of the new government building. The deck of the Etruria sloped about as greatly as Courthouse hill. At one moment it would face due north, and the next due south. In the smoking saloon things were of a lively and varied character. Ever and anon, spittoons, camp-stools, chess-men, gin-slings, boys, whiskey toddies, stewards and passengers would be all in a pile at one end of the saloon, and the next moment they would radiate to the four corners at a 2:40 gait. A young man came whizzing by Captain Lee, spun across the saloon and brought up against the other side of it with a horrible gash across his head, a broken arm, and a bruised body. Captain Lee started to his relief as he lay on the floor, and you would have thought he had been fired from a catapult if you could have seen him wrap his sound arm around a pillar in the centre of the saloon, while his body swung straight out, and then downward, like the sweep of a whip-lash, and there he "anchored."

On the 4th, at 6 P. M., the Irish coast came into full view on our left. The rugged grandeur of its tall rock cliff rising abruptly from the water reminded me forcibly of the James river at Balcony Falls.

Just in front of the position of our ship, a mile or more from the coast stood, in solitary grandeur, an immense rock, on which is built Facinet lighthouse.

Our trip has been the quickest ever made across the Atlantic by about two hours. Think of it, ye Lynchburgers, that your fellow-citizens have been participants in so distinguished an honor. Our party have all proven good sailors. Every one of us, without an exception, have eaten five square meals every day. True, it was sometimes attended with difficulty, as we had to watch the water bottles, salt cellars, etc., as they flew around promiscuously. We could make sure only, on some occasions, of such things as we could keep our fingers on. While our ship was very rapid she was an adept at "rolling," and sad havoc was wrought among our passengers on the 2d and 3d in the matter of "casting up accounts." Personally, however, in this connection I was prepared to exclaim, *Vedi, vidi, vici!*

LETTER II.

LOOKING OVER LIVERPOOL—CHARACTER OF THE BUILDINGS—IMPRESSIONS OF THE PEOPLE—VISITS A TOBACCO FACTORY IN WHICH THE WEED IS COOKED—A PROBLEM IN FINANCE—CONVENIENCES FOR HUNGRY TRAVELERS.

BRISTOL, ENG., Sept. 11, 1885.

My Dear Boy:

In the interval since sending you a batch of jumbled notes, taken hurriedly, we have been looking over Liverpool. The immense quantity of stone and glass used here is almost the first thing that attracted my attention. About one-half of the inside partitions in our hotel and the dividing walls between the rooms are of very thick ground glass. A greater portion of the railroad stations are of stone, iron and glass. You see these materials everywhere.

The appearance of the people here is decidedly more like those in a Virginia city than are those of our nearer neighbors, the New Yorkers. We have seen a number of very fine buildings, and a few days ago heard in front of one of them, St. George's Hall, several very incendiary addresses from members of a gathering purporting to be composed of workingmen. Of liberty of speech there seemed a superabundance, and judging from the occasion indicated, an Englishman need not go out of his own country to enjoy it.

I went through a large tobacco factory in Liverpool on Wednesday, and as a matter of more than ordinary interest to the average Lynchburger, will try to give you an idea of what I saw, which was as strange to me as though I had not been reared in one of the greatest tobacco manufacturing towns in the world. I was first taken into a room about 50 by 150 feet in its dimensions, where there was a number of girls engaged in stemming leaf tobacco, which had been cased until it was perfectly supple. I was then conducted into another, where the strip was being made into coils or ropes, ranging in size from the little finger to the arm. In another apartment these coils were put into shapes called targets, ranging in size from about that of a kegshead down to the thickness of a collar box. These shapes were put into baking pans and baked in large ovens, and after being taken out and allowed to cool off, were wrapped around with hemp rope on the round side, set on flat iron sheets and put under hydraulic pressure; after which they are taken out, boxed and shipped to the retailer. All tobacco used here, certainly all manufactured here, goes through a cooking or baking process. The duty on the raw stock is 3s. and 6d., yet the manufactured article can be and is sold for 3s. and 3d. Think of that, 6 cents less than the duty! Upon what principle of legitimate profits can this be accounted for?

I am staying at a hotel here, St. Vincent's Rocks, which is high upon a rocky hill or mountain somewhat in shape like that of a sugar loaf, at the foot of which flows the Avon river. I can see in front of me for many miles over the county of Somerset, and on my left and in the rear an equal distance into Gloustershire.

I came down from Liverpool yesterday, 198 miles, in 5 hours, and go to London to morrow by the "Flying Dutchman," which makes the trip in 2½ hours. While traveling by cars one can telegraph ahead free of expense, and have a delightfully hot meal handed into your carriage at any station on the line. The lunch is placed in a square willow basket, with plate, glass, knife, fork, salt, pepper, butter, etc. I have always found, on such occasions, a nice salad of some kind and a bottle of wine, stout, lager, ale or mineral water in the basket accompanying the food; the cost is 3s. for cold, or 3s. 6d. for a hot meal with the trimmings indicated.

LETTER III.

A GLIMPSE OF BREMEN—THE RASKT-KELLER WINE CEL-
LARS—MEETING OLD ACQUAINTANCES—THE PICTURES
OF BREMEN—A TRIP ACROSS THE GERMAN OCEAN—RE-
TURN TO LONDON.

MORLES HOTEL,
LONDON, ENG., Sept 27, 1885.

My Dear Boy:

Since sending a card from the continent, written in Raskt-Keller, one of the most famous wine cellars in the world, I have returned to London, where I was rejoiced to meet Messrs. R. H. T. Adams, Dr. Thornhill and Davis Christian. Mr. Adams is in the possession of enviable health, while Dr. Thornhill says he is daily increasing in vigor. Mr. Halsey and wife and Capt. Lee leave for Scotland to-morrow; and Mr. Moorman sails for home in a day or two. Messrs. Adams, Thornhill, Christian and the writer go hence to Scotland on Wednesday.

It is perhaps pertinent at this point to say something of Bremen, from whence I have so recently come. The old city was built about the year 818, and was originally a walled town with a wide, deep moat entirely encircling it, which, in the progress of the centuries, has deepened and widened until it now forms a beautiful sheet of clear water some two miles in circumference. The new city has been built around the outer circle. The gigantic statue of Rolland, an ancient knight who performed wondrous deeds with sword and lance, stands near the City Hall, a building in the older city whose existence dates back for about five centuries. On the wall of this ancient structure is an immense painting representing Solomon's judgment, when the two women claimed the child. The latter is held aloft by a soldier who is represented as being almost in the act of smiting the child in twain. The dates on this picture indicate that it was painted in 1353, and twice retouched. They are as follows: "1353"—retouched in 1582, and again in 1615. Another picture of recent date hangs on the opposite wall, representing a regiment of Bremen soldiers engaged in battle with a French regiment in the late Franco-Prussian war. The picture is a very fine one.

The famous wine cellar, Raskt-Kellar,* is beneath this building; the main cellar, fitted up with tables, stalls and alcoves for its customers, is about 200 feet long by 75 wide. The wine is stored in other rooms. Two or three times a day a guide accompanies visit-

---

*A card of the character here referred to was sent to the editor of one of the Lynchburg daily papers and was reproduced with an introduction in his journal as follows:

"COSTLY WINE.—Our townsman, R. L. Miller, Esq., now in Europe, sends us a lithograph card upon which he writes: 'This card is written in the Raskt-Keller, the most celebrated wine vault in the German Empire. This picture represents the Bacchus cask, filled in 1624. We have just taken a drink of it. The value of the wine, with compound interest, is 5,500 marks a drop.'"

ors through the rooms, explaining the contents to them. The first one we entered contains 12 casks, each holding 15,000 bottles of wine. These casks represent the 12 apostles including Judas, and contain the best wine. An immense cask, with a beautifully carved figure of Bacchus astride the head, holds 25,000 bottles. Another room contains no wine, but on the ceiling is painted a large red rose. It was formerly used by the old City Council for secret meetings, whence doubtless originated the expression "*sub rosa.*" These cellars are owned and run by the city. The doors are promptly closed at 11 o'clock P. M., and the supply of wine ceases at exactly 12, midnight. You can order as much as you please up to this hour, and spend the night in drinking it, but should your supply become exhausted after 12, no more can be had for love or money.

We had a very pleasant trip across the German Ocean on our way back, landing at Flushing, in Holland, and thence returning to Queenstown, England. Yesterday Messrs. Adams, Thornhill, Christian and myself visited St. Paul's Cathedral, the oldest church in London. We also paid a visit to the International Industrial Exhibition. Of course Westminster Abbey came in for a share of our attention, where we saw among other things the old monuments erected to all of England's departed kings and queens, and to England's celebrated dead in other ranks than those of rulers. There were numerous artists present during our visit copying the grand old monuments and beautifully carved stone arches. We failed to gain admission to the Parliament building, as this is the period of recess and the building was consequently closed.

I have seen so many things, and so little of any of them, that I am at a loss about what to write. Messrs. Adams, Thornhill and Christian will sail from Glasgow for Bremen, and thence on to Paris, etc. The writer will go from Edinburgh to Liverpool, and from there sail for home.

LETTER IV.

NEW YORK TO LIVERPOOL—A ROUGH PASSAGE—THE "STIRRING" SEA SICKNESS—APPALLING WEATHER—OLD NEPTUNE ON A VERITABLE BENDER.

R. M. S. "GERMANIC,"
August 31, 1887.

My Dear Boy:

After an interregnum of nearly two years, I am again on the briny deep and amid very unpropitious surroundings as to the fickle winds and waves. We sailed promptly at one minute past 10 o'clock A. M., Wednesday, August 24. From the very incipiency of the voyage we have had bad weather; the 25th it rained, and we had stiff winds; the same continued on the 26th, and notwithstanding C. was as fresh as a lark, Col. Bullock was very limp and sickish, and the writer was sick all over. The following colloquy occurred in our state-room:

Col. B. "What makes the ship roll so, confound her? She hasn't been still a minute since we left Sandy Hook. Is sea-sickness from the brain or stomach?"

M. "Both, has been my experience."

The waves increase in size and number, and as a sequence in a few hours the Colonel and myself are too sick to think and too busy to talk. The night of the 27th the wind increased to a hurricane, the waves continually rolling over the deck. Sail after sail is hoisted to keep the ship steady, but they are split into ribbons as they are put up. Three of our boats are seriously damaged, the partition around the lookout blown away and the decks fairly swimming in a depth of water. Everything is damp and sticky; the smell of bilge-water, the odor from the smoke-room and kitchen permeate every part of the ship, while a large majority of our passengers are confined to their berths. Those who can move about, look like moulting chickens, and would show well at a wake, but would be sadly out of place on any more festive occasion. C. is one of the very few who remain disgustingly well, horribly cheerful and chronically hungry. Col. B. and the writer lay, or rather roll, from side to side in our berths listening to the shrieking of the wind through the cordage of the vessel, the swish of the seething waters, as it races past, and the dull thud of the bow as she thumps through wave after wave.

The night of the 27th, although we are so little past midsummer, is as dark as January. Intervals of a groping twilight alternate with seasons of utter blackness, and it is impossible to trace the reason of these changes in the flying horrors of the sky. The wind blows the breath out of one's nostrils; all heaven seems to thunder overhead like the flapping of one huge sail in the tempest, and when there falls a momentary lull on board, we can hear the gusts dismally sweeping in the distance. Looking over the side of the vessel we peer upon a world of blackness, where the waters wheel and boil, where the waves joust together with the noise of an explosion, and the foam towers and vanishes in the twinkling of an eye. The fury, height and transiency of their spouting is a thing to be seen, not considered or described. During this fearful storm one of our steerage passengers adds another to the list. A purse of four pounds and ten shillings is made up, and we name it " Hurricane."

C. sighted a vessel to-day (the 30th) and assures us that she is *anchored*. The fun comes in when it is remembered that the water is only *seven miles* deep just around here. The Colonel to-day expresses fear lest our outside cabin be washed overboard. The writer is just beginning to feel a little interest in life again. Will probably sight the Irish coast some time to-night (1st) and will mail this letter in Queenstown to-morrow.

LETTER V.

ARRIVAL IN LIVERPOOL—THE WONDERFUL DOCKS—A LABOR-SAVING MERCHANT—DUBLIN—A PLEASANT VISIT TO BRAY—A WELL-TRAINED HORSE—IRISH NATURE.

LIVERPOOL, Sept. 16, 1887.

My Dear Boy:

We found upon our arrival here that "Mexican Joe" and his troupe were the all-absorbing topic. A girl from his show galloping down Church street to-day at break-neck speed attracted unwonted attention. I noticed that the older people stopped and watched her as long as she was in sight, while hundreds of young men and boys ran after the pony.

One of the most wonderful examples of construction in the world consists in the docks of this city. The largest ocean steamer can be dry-docked here. We saw the "British King" during our visit to them in the Alexandria dock, undergoing repairs to her propeller. A walk along the dock-wall, which extends for several miles, affords one an idea of what is susceptible of being done in the way of massive masonry by a people who have subjected all of the elements contained in it to the attainment of their own purposes, whether commercial or otherwise.

I visited a store here, known as Lewis', that exceeds even Yankee thrift and ingenuity in the adaptation of labor-saving appliances. The employees are numbered by hundreds and the business averages £1,500 daily. One clerk sits in a kind of pulpit above the counter, while just in front of him is a perfect network of little railroads running in different directions to the counters of other clerks—some twenty or thirty in number. Calling at the soap counter, I purchased a package of three cakes of plain soap, for which the charge was twenty cents, giving a two shilling piece to the salesman, who put it into a hollow ball, placed the latter on one of the railroads and sped it away to the clerk in the pulpit—the correct change came back in the ball to the soap counter.

With a view of visiting the Lakes of Killarney and other points of interest in Ireland, we went first to Dublin from this city, arrived in the night and stopped at a very inferior hotel. True, we had chickens, but they were not such as would have impelled an itinerant preacher at home to have left his devotions; on the other hand they were unattractive, ancient fellows, whose leg muscles, preternaturally developed by a long career of fruitless scratching, defied the teeth of even our hungry party. We also had a loud-flavored ham in paper crinolettes, together with tongues of leather-like consistency, all flanked by stony-hearted cold bread and environed by a forbidding regiment of evil-looking decanters of poteen. Our party, however, notwithstanding such temptations to ill-humor, are full of eager anticipation, rendering the Colonel so absent-minded or oblivious to surrounding objects, that at breakfast this morning he put soy on his eggs, and buttered the newspaper instead of his toast.

I came near forgetting to mention a pleasant trip to Bray, behind a team of four fine horses hitched to a "tally-ho" coach, owned by a friend of the writer, and by him put at our disposal. Bray is twenty miles from Dublin. We made the trip in two and a quarter hours, supplemented by a fine lunch, after which we took a promenade on the esplanade on the sea wall, which runs for miles up and down the beach, and which is beyond question the most beautiful walk I ever beheld. The place was full—all the old ladies having fans, umbrellas and vinaigrettes; all of the younger ones rejoiced in sailor hats, cotton frocks, sunshades and the latest novel; all of the old gentlemen were arrayed in white duck and pith helmets, while all of the younger ones were ensconced in boating flannels, tennis stripes or lightest of checks. Every nursemaid had secured a sweetheart, and every child a sand-spade or a sunstroke. I passed one old lady sound asleep, her face wreathed in smiles, doubtless from pleasant dreams, and at her feet lay a novel on its stomach in the sand. As far as the eye could reach the broad blue Irish Sea lay glittering beyond the emerald cliffs. The promenade was crowded with well-dressed people, and the cheery thud of the lawn-tennis ball against its racket and the laughter of the players sounded and mingled in harmony with the never-ending plash of the waves. Bray is a green spot in memory.

Our coach made the trip back to Dublin in two and a half hours, when we went to dine with an Irish gentleman of the old school—a friend of the writer, and I believe a kinsman. A beautiful lawn and grove, comprised of forty acres, leads up to the fine but very old house, with its large halls and rooms and wide porches of stone and marble. After an hour spent in the garden and shrubbery, dinner was announced. My entertainer's wife, who, by the way, is the daughter of a baronet, was absent in London, and her sister with her two little girls did the honors. We had sherry, champagne and other wines freely; then the ladies retired, when we had hot water and Irish whiskey. Then it was that the shades of Charles O'Malley materialized. The party was composed of Col. Mapleson, the husband of "Marie Rose," the most celebrated singer in this country, with Mr. Childs, our host, Col. Bullock, my friend's partner, and the writer. Colonel M. proposed to bet that Mr. ——'s horse could not, or would not, come into the dining-room and prove himself gentle and kind. The bet was promptly taken and two grooms ordered to bring the horse in. In a few moments we heard his iron shod hoofs on the marble step, and the next moment he was in the room, a coal-black hunter and a beautiful animal. After he had shown his paces around the tables, our host, Mr. M——, mounted him and made him place his two fore-feet in a chair, remarking that he could ride him up three flights of steps into the drawing-room on the second floor. Col. Bullock very promptly stepped forward and earnestly craved this privilege, which was granted, and right gallantly did my countryman perform his task. The first flight of steps was quickly mounted and a stop made on the broad landing, when the old gentleman and his magnificent black threw up their heads with a conscious look of pride; then quickly ascending to the second and third landing, the Colonel rode proudly into the ladies drawing-room. You may rest assured it created quite a flutter. Colonel B. is to-day the proudest man in Great Britain, and we correspondingly reflect his grandeur. After this episode we decided it would be best to return to our hotel, as jumping the horse over the table was in serious contemplation. It is more than possible that some of our more uncharitable friends, in view of the foregoing statements, may jump at hasty conclusions and are ready to exclaim, "They were drunk." Go easy, my dear friends; if this be your conclusion, you are mistaken. Know ye not, that there is something in the very air the people of Ireland breathe that renders them ever ready for the commission of dare-devil deeds, and I now know that Lever did not exaggerate one particle in his delineation of this characteristic of his countrymen.

I purposed to say something about our trip to the Lakes of Killarney and of the desolation of the "evicted" farms, which are numerous in this section, as well as of the beggars—such beggars, such persistent, such patient, hearty, cheerful beggars—but I have already written too much and must say good-bye. All of our party are well. Mr. C. has turned into an exclamation point and Col. Bullock is almost rejuvenated. I continue to maintain my equable poise, but find my thoughts perpetually turning homeward, and my constant wish is that the faces of my friends and dear ones may be like the daughter of Egypt—a face that age could not wither or change; a slight case of the blues, you perceive.

LETTER VI.

MANCHESTER—ART EXHIBITION—A MAGNIFICENT DISPLAY—RAMBLES IN EDINBURGH—JENNIE DEAN'S COTTAGE, HOLYROOD AND VARIOUS OTHER PLACES OF INTEREST—BILLINGSGATE AND A FISH DINNER.

LONDON, Sept. 23, 1887.

My Dear Boy:

In a former letter I neglected to make mention of our visit to the exhibition at Manchester, near Liverpool. The picture galleries contain more oil paintings of celebrity than were ever gathered together before. Only think of sixteen or eighteen of Landseer's best creations, together with a number of Long's, Wallace's and Millet's wonderfully touching and pathetic picturing. The most beautiful of these, in my judgment, is one entitled " The Poor Man's Friend," representing a fisherman at his cottage door mending a net; his wife stands in the door and his little girl is leaning on his knee; at his side stands a blind beggar, while the mendicant's little girl is bashfully and tearfully pleading for a penny. The attitude of eager pleading in the child's face and position is something marvelous, and would touch the heart of the most callous. Another fine picture by C. W. Mitchell is " Hypatia," Charles Kingsley's heroine.

"On up the nave, fresh shreds of her dress strewing the holy pavements—up to the altar—right underneath the great, still Christ, and even there those hell-hounds paused.

"She shook herself free from her tormentors, and springing back rose for one moment to her full height, naked, snow-white against the dusky mass around. Shame and indignation in those wild, clear eyes, but not a stain of fear. Her lips were open to speak, but the words that should have come from them reached God's ear alone, for in an instant Peter struck her down."

Lady E. Butler's painting of the return of the gallant six hundred from their charge at Balaklava is exhibited by the owner, John Whitehead, Esq. "M'liss," by Long, and "The Village Wedding," by Luke Fildes. The painting of "The Kit Kat Klub,", by Yeames, and L. Almatadema's realistic marble work, Millard's "Bride of Lammermoor," from which so many copies have been taken, and from which so many engravings have been made, are all here, and richly deserving of close attention To even attempt to mention a few of the 2104 paintings and sculptures would require a week.

While in Edinburgh we visited the castle and the historical old Abbey and palace of Holyrood;. the next day riding over to Arthur's seat, passing Jennie Dean's cottage and underneath the Salisbury crags —Sir Walter Scott's favorite walk—and where, it is said, he composed "The Heart of Midlothian." In the evening we went down to that wonderful piece of engineering skill, the bridge across the Firth of Forth. An idea of the immensity of the work may be obtained from the fact that 4,000 men have been employed here for five years, and it will require two more years to complete the work. The bridge, with its approaches, is one and three-quarters miles long, and the spans are 1,750 feet, built on the cantalever plan.

Back in London, we have spent five busy days in sight-seeing. Took in the Abbey and Tower, and then spent a day at Kensington Museum, where can be seen representatives of every animal (man included), bird, fish, fowl, tree, shrub, flower, mineral, insect—in fact of everything that has lived or died since Noah's day. Madam Taussard's wax-works were a source of great enjoyment to Col. B. and J. C. I am the guide, having gone over these grounds before, and consequently essay the role of "Ferguson." At Madame Taussard's, Mr. C. and Col. B. walked up to the wax figure of a policeman and insisted on its answering some questions. The crowd saw the fun and quickly gathered around them. They soon saw their mistake and fled to me. I saw a huge amount of embarrassment, and promptly declined to recognize either of them when they spoke to me. I pretended not to know them from Adam, and they were mean enough not to like my very proper conduct. Yesterday we visited Scotland Yard and then went down to Billingsgate and had a fish dinner at the "Three Tuns Tavern," consisting of six kinds of fish, viz: cod, eels, brill, haddock, soles, turbot, with anchovy, oyster, clam and mussel sauces. The tavern stands just back of the fish market, the latter constituting a rare sight to our party. Every kind of edible fish is here offered for sale, from a half-pound to a hundred-pounder. C. F., the K.'s and Uncles Charles and George B. would open their eyes at the number, size and variety of the finny tribe here exhibited.

Our lady friends at home would have greatly enjoyed a visit to the building in which the Queen's Jubilee presents are displayed. They came from every quarter of the globe. The inhabitants of the Sandwich Islands, Heligoland, Australasia, Canada, India, China, residents in the colonies, English residents in Seville, consuls on the continent, all united their gifts with those at home.

LETTER VII.

BEAUTIFUL PARIS—ITS NUMEROUS PLACES OF INTEREST AND BEAUTY—THE MORGUE—GOBELIN TAPESTRY—BRUSSELS AND ITS CATHEDRAL—A LEGEND CONNECTED WITH IT.

BRUXELLES, Oct. 3, 1887.

My Dear Boy:

We left Belgium two days ago, and as our trip through Belgium, Holland and Germany will be a very rapid one, Col. B. decided to remain with Mr. Boykin and his family. They are Virginians, and the brief time we spent with them will be long remembered as one of the most pleasant incidents in our travels.

Beautiful Paris! It is not within the power of pen to describe thy countless attractions and beauties; certainly mine is incompetent to the task of affording even a shadow of the substantive of them—they must be seen to be appreciated. In visiting the superb palaces and enchanting gardens, and the galleries of painting and sculpture, we felt for the time being that we were in possession of Aladdin's lamp. The palace of Versailles was especially attractive, being a marvel of art in its decorations and furnishings, with grounds that are extensive and artistically laid out. It is needless, however, to particularize, but to afford you an idea of how much we did see in a few days will only mention a few of the many places visited: The great Boulevards, Porte St. Denis, Palace de la Republique, the Bastile, Rue Rivoli, Louvre, St. Germain, l'Auxerrois, Bourse, Palais Royal, Champs Elysees, Arc de Triomphe, St. Augustine, Grand Opera House, (where we saw the "Huguenots" and the "Patriot" performed, the ballet being composed of over six hundred girls on the stage at one time), Place Vendome, Tuilleries Gardens, Place du Carrousel, Notre Dame, Tomb of Napoleon—and Napoleons are everywhere, the people worshipping the very name of their dead hero. Louis the XIV. is also a very important personage with all Parisians. I visited the Morgue alone, none of our party desiring to accompany me. Three dead bodies were on the marble slabs. One presented a horrible appearance, the face being terribly battered. The other two were men and suicides—one having ended his career through drowning, the other by hanging. A visit to the Gobelin Tapestry works was very interesting; only one and one-half inches by each man being done per day. I saw no women employed in the works, which are owned and operated by the government. The Column Vendome is a marvel of art. The tall circular shaft was cast from fourteen hundred bronze guns captured by Napoleon.

The portion of France through which we passed from Dieppe to Paris is low, exhibiting a great deal of wet land, with innumerable rows of poplar and willow trees fringing a multitude of streams and canals. No better or more beautiful description of the country could be expressed than is contained in the following little gem of a poem entitled " Petit Chauson Picard ":

> Pale leaves waver and whisper low,
>   (Silvered leaves of the poplar tree),
> Waters wander and billows blow
>   In Picardie.
>
> Misty green of the orchard grass,
>   Grass-grown lanes by the sedge-fringed lea,
> Pleasant ways for the feet that pass
>   Through Picardie
>
> Here the youth on a blue May night,
>   Soft to his maiden's home steals he,
> Binds a bough to the lintel's height
>   Of dark fir tree.
>
> Gaston sigheth for Bernadette!
>   (Sorrow to come—or joy to be?)
> This she knows by the token set
>   In secrecy.
>
> Long lagoons where the lilies lie,
>   (Blossoms and buds of ivory),
> Sweet the meadows and fair the sky
>   Of Picardie!
>
> Where be the waters to drown regret?
>   Where be the leaves of sleep's own tree?
> Nowhere else in the world—nor yet
>   In Picardie.

The only impediment to our pleasure in France has been in a lack of sunshine and a superabundance of rain.

Our advent into Brussels, the capital of the small kingdom of Belgium, was greeted with the genial rays of the sun, the beautiful god of light being out in all his glory. How delightfully his warm rays flow into my window and bathe my chilled frame. What would the world be worth—or man himself—if its light or warmth were withdrawn from us? Heart and brain and soul would shrivel, sicken and die in the monotonous gloom, for sunshine is the revivifying power of nature—indeed, the motive principle. "And God said, let there be light, and there was light." A visit to the cathedral at Brussels was first in order. It is one of the finest in Europe. The carved wood pulpit, said to be the most elaborate piece of wood carving in the world, was presented to this church by Marie Theresa in 1776. At the base are seen life-size figures of Adam and Eve driven by angels from Paradise; on the left, Death is represented as pursuing them. The figures of Adam and Eve are so grouped as to support the globe, which is placed above them, and in the concavity of which the preacher stands. This globe rests upon a tree, on whose summit is a canopy supported by two angels, assisted in their task by Truth in the form of a female figure. Below are seen the Holy Family and infant Jesus, the latter standing upon a crescent and holding a cross, with the aid of which and his mother he crushes the serpent's head. Below the pulpit are two small staircases, and on the trunks of the trees—which form the balustrade—are to be seen various animals. On the side of Adam an ostrich and an eagle; on that of Eve the *peacock*, the *parrot* and the ape. A part of the cathedral was built to commemorate a miracle which runs as follows: Some 350 years ago the French overran this country, and wherever they went everything in church and home was carried off. One of the priests of the cathedral, knowing the fate of the altar furniture of other churches, hid the gold and jewels of this sanctuary in a wall on the west side of the building. Just as the work was finished and the last coat of lime had been spread on the wall concealing it, the French entered the building. Not finding anything of value where so much was expected, they very promptly killed the priest. The bishop, on hearing that the French had secured nothing, surmised that the vessels had been hidden somewhere within the cathedral. Years of search, however, proved fruitless. One of the priests in charge of the building now decided to devote his life to prayer in order that the lost treasure might be found. After years and years consecrated to that end, and while praying one morning with his face to the west wall of the building, he saw a bright gush of sunlight pour from an aperture in the wall—the regular orb was then shining on the other side of the immense structure. Workmen were at once summoned and the plaster removed from the wall, when all of the vessels and jewels were revealed and removed from where they had so long been in hiding. A chapel and an immense memorial window, illustrative of the miracle, now stand where the wall once stood.

Probably the finest modern building in the world is the court-house in this place. The architect died under the mental strain incident to preparing the plans and superintending the building. The widow was awarded a pension of 10,000 francs. Some of the young lawyers were promenading the halls during our visit, amusing me no little with their showy black gowns trimmed with white fur. Everybody here wear uniforms, and the lower the office the more gold lace.

A curiosity of Brussels, and one seen by few strangers, is the statue of a little boy perfectly nude, and used by the neighbors as a fountain from which they get their water for all purposes. He is called Menneken P. He stands at the corner of two streets, Rue du Cliene and Rue de l'Eluve. This little fellow was a Burgundian under the Duke of B——, a German under Maximillian, a Spaniard under Charles V., Rebel during the Netherland troubles, Austrian under Maria Theresa, Republican in 1794, French under Napoleon, semi-Dutch under William, and is now Belgian under Leopold. Every one in Brussels knows the man or child of bronze, one cubit high— alone, without wings, and consequently fixed where he stands. He is fixed upon an ornamental pedestal of much taste. His natural state is one of nakedness, but during the grand festivals of Brussels he is dressed as a noble, lord, knight or soldier. The history of Menneken P. as related by our guide is this: The fountain of Menneken P. was erected by a rich burgess of Brussels, who, having lost during a festival his much-beloved and only child, three or four years old, found him the fifth day afterwards at the spot where the statue now stands, and in the identical posture in which he is here represented. There are many other legends about this very interesting little fellow, but the above is believed to be the true one.

We will be in Holland to-morrow and Germany next day. This, with other letters, needs to be charitably considered, for the reason that my mind is in such a dazed condition from sight-seeing, and everything is in such a jumble, that I find it difficult to follow an idea—when one strikes me—an inch, before I switch off at right angles on something else.

LETTER VIII.

HOLLAND—THE WERTZ MUSEUM AT AMSTERDAM—A BRIEF NOTICE OF SOME OF THE REMARKABLE WORKS OF ART CONTAINED IN IT—DIAMOND CUTTERS—ROTTERDAM A CITY OF CANALS AND WOODEN SHOES.

AMSTERDAM, Oct. 8, 1887.

My Dear Boy:

The most interesting collection of oil paintings we have seen is that in the Wertz Museum at Brussels. "Ouida" says of Wertz: "Are there not many to whom his name is yet as an empty sound, telling nothing? I fear so. He gave his whole life for fame, and yet fame has only shed upon him a fitful and incomplete luster." Wertz was born in 1805, in the old town of Diant, on the banks of the river Meuse. His best picture, in my judgment, is "The Greeks and Trojans contending for the body of Patroclus." The central figures are the beautiful nude corpse of Patroclus and a divine fury endeavoring to drag it to the Grecian camp. The latter is aided in this purpose by a throng of Grecian warriors, while the Trojans struggle to bear the body away to the city. It is doubtful whether a more beautiful representation of a dead man was ever presented on canvass than is seen in this picture. "The Triumph of Christ" comes next; it was painted in an unused factory in Brussels, and fairly shares with his "Patroclus" the honor of being his best work. "The Orphans" represents the dead body of the father being removed from the humble cottage. The wife, or rather widow, still young, leans in gloom against the wall; the children, utterly unconscious of the nature of death, and not understanding the removal of "father," fly like a band of beautiful young furies to attack, with cries, blows and kicks, the men lifting up the coffin. The picture is most intense; one can almost fancy the screams of the children sounding in one's ears.

I can mention only a few more of these wonderful pictures. Among them, "The Revolt of Hell," fifty by thirty feet. Here are huge demons writhing in every imaginable contortion; avalanches of rocks hurling into the bottomless pit; the entombment in the central panel is a representation of that event as set forth in the Gospel. The conception of Satan in this painting is remarkable, and I think correct. No human form more beautiful can be conceived; the evil is in his look; the eyes alone, "those mirrors of the soul," betray his fiendish intentions. The most remarkable of his modern subjects is the "Burnt Child." This represents a poor woman who has gone out to buy provisions, and finds on her return the cradle on fire and the poor baby dead. She is represented as just having snatched the little body from the flames and examining, in a dazed way, its dreadful injuries. "Buried Alive," "Hunger," "Madness," "Crime," and "The Suicide," are among the most remarkable of this very interesting gallery. That of "The Suicide" is especially so. It represents a young man who has destroyed himself. The body is tottering to its fall. On either side of him is his good angel and his bad; the former veils its face in sorrow and compassion, while a laugh of fiendish glee lights up the face of the latter, who holds a second pistol, should the first fail; on a table close by a materialistic volume is lying, together with "A Scene in Hell," Quasemodo, (see Victor Hugo's Notre Dame de Paris); "Two Young Girls, or the Beautiful Rosine"; "Old Nick's Mirror" and "The Man of the Future Regarding the Things of the Past," (the men of the future are to be giants of civilization as compared to the people of our day), completes the most attractive of this very interesting gallery.

AMSTERDAM AND ROTTERDAM.

Rotterdam, to which we paid a brief visit, is a city of canals and wooden shoes, where the dogs and women do all the work. Our guide here proved to be quite a character. After walking about for an hour he suggested we get a carriage. We agreed. He went off and soon came back with two fine black horses hitched to a very fine carriage, for which we paid a very fine price. When the hour for luncheon arrived, the scamp took us to the most expensive " cafe" in the place and ordered for himself the most expensive dishes, for which we had to pay. At Amsterdam we went to see the diamond cutters. There are over 12,000 men engaged in that business in that city. The diamonds are lovely, but quite high even here. The Palace, the Crystal Palace and the Museum, with innumerable other attractions, we " took in " in Amsterdam. Now for Bremen and London and Liverpool, thence home.

LETTER IX.

LEAVING EUROPE — BRIEF OBSERVATIONS ON THE TRIP — IRELAND—FRANCE—HOLLAND—GERMANY, &C.—VISIT TO DR. MORILL MACKENZIE—MEETING AN OLD ACQUAINTANCE—HOMEWARD BOUND.

LONDON, Oct. 10, 1887.

My Dear Boy:

This epistle, which will be brief, is begun, as indicated by the date line, in England's greatest city, but will be concluded with the arrival of our steamer in America's greatest city, New York. I have engaged passage by the Guion steamship "Alaska," for the 14th inst. A brief reference to some of the countries we have seen, and people we have met on this trip, may not be inappropriate at this point.

The south of Ireland is in a woeful condition, while the north, or Protestant portion of the country is as prosperous as any part of our own dear land. The causes that have produced this effect you can figure out at your leisure. By the way, there is a queer couplet on one of the old churches in Dublin, which is credited to Dean Swift. The Dean wrote on the door of the edifice indicated the following.

> "Turk, Jew or Atheist
> Can enter here, but not a Papist."

The Dean's servant, a good Catholic, saw the lines

and turned the tables on his worship in the following neat manner:

> "He who wrote this wrote it well
> But the same is written on the door of hell."

Paris is the queen of the world, but France and the French people were a woeful disappointment to us all. Brussels is a marvel of beauty, and all Belgium looks well.

Holland and its people are both queer and quaint, presenting many points of interest to the traveller. The inhabitants are slow but pains taking, and in the main, intelligent and thrifty. We saw no beggars in Holland.

Germany has the appearance of one large park, with its fine highways and well-conducted railroads, telegraphs, &c., all of which are in the hands of the government.

In Bremen the writer met many of his good friends, and again found himself in the "Raskt Kellar" doing homage to the little god Bacchus. A quick run brought us back to Flushing, and soon we were again in old England, and very glad we were to hear our native language spoken. I never intend to learn any other, for the reason that I do not wish to encourage foreigners in their conceit of speaking anything but the English tongue. If we fail to learn their language, they must of necessity learn ours. While in Liverpool on the 12th we had quite a pleasant surprise. Walking down Church street I saw a familiar figure in front of us, and to our great pleasure we were soon shaking hands with Mr. Richard Mathews, of old Lynchburg. Mr. M. will sail with us on the "Alaska," which he informs us is a good vessel, and he ought to know, if the fiftieth voyage he has made be considered. While in London the writer called on the celebrated Dr. Morill MacKenzie, and for the benefit of Lynchburg doctors, that they may learn the value of five or ten minutes of time expended professionally, tell them that I paid four guineas, or $20, each visit. I only indulged twice. Colonel Bullock will sail on the "Brittania," the 19th, in company with Messrs. Boykin and Mayo, of Richmond.

In due time (14th) our party was on board the "Alaska," with a smooth sea, balmy air and the prospect of a delightful run. Our passenger list shows two celebrities—Mrs. Scott Siddons and Archibald Forbes, the correspondent of the *London Times* during our civil war. We also have a few of the "Mexican Joe" company. There are 200 cabin and 600 steerage passengers on board. From the very inception of the voyage the weather and the waters have been all that could be desired. These indispensable adjuncts, together with a jolly company, and bright anticipations of soon seeing the dear ones at home and the many good friends of the old "burg," rendered things extremely pleasant. From all this, however, we were rudely awakened on the 22d by the wind blowing big guns and rendering thereby two-thirds of our passengers sick. The most of them have turned a beautiful greenish yellow, and look as limp as a string. Two ladies fainted, while the writer dare not move even a finger for fear of again being sick. We have averaged to noon to-day about 400 miles; will sight Fire Island light in the morning, and encounter the custom house officials about noon. This will be about the eighth time these fellows will have gone through us. In summing up the chief characteristics of the vessels in which it has been my fortune to encounter the waves of the Atlantic, it may be said that as a first-class roller give me the " Etruria," of the Cunard line; as a pitcher from base, I will always back the "City of Rome," of the Anchor line; and as a good boat for a funeral occasion, or any other slow ceremony, I would take the "Germanic," White Star line. I find the "Alaska" combines all the qualities of the other three, except she is quicker in her rolls and more reckless in her pitches.

Messrs. Childs and Mathews think this sort of weather is fun I can't see it in that way, I am sorry to say.

LETTER X.

BY WAY OF PROLOGUE—EN ROUTE TO AUSTRALIA AS COMMISSIONER TO THE MELBOURNE EXPOSITION—NOTES BY THE WAY—THE ROMANCE OF A WHISKEY BOTTLE—ARRIVAL IN DENVER.

DENVER, COLO., June 24, 1888.

My Dear Boy:

I might preface this my first letter, resultant from the trip now in progress, with some observations upon the difficulty every traveler meets in obtaining accurate information outside of guide-books, or where guide-books are not available, and the consequent temptation to plagiarize more or less whenever a favorable opportunity is afforded. If what I shall write of my experiences and observation is not always wholly original—and I cannot promise that every line of it will be—I am sure you will be the gainer thereby.

After leaving the hills of Lynchburg behind us, nothing new or noteworthy occurred until we reached Chattanooga, where we spent two days looking for lost baggage. A visit to Lookout Mountain and trip to the top on the cable cars was a revelation to my fellow-traveler and myself. The incline is fully 75 degrees, and I would estimate the distance to the top at about a half or three-fourths of a mile. The cars are about the size of those used upon our streets that are propelled by mule or horse power. We observed in getting aboard that the cars were provided with a cow-catcher in front and rear. After starting John asks: "Mr. Conductor, is it possible you need a cow-catcher on a road as steep as this? Why, a goat could scarcely climb up here!" "Oh yes," replied the conductor, "we find it useful in shoving the mountain cows off the track." Both John and myself are both as quiet as mice for a brief time after this episode, but on nearing the top, a few minutes later, my companion "got even." There, standing close to the track, was a mountain cow engaged in pensively chewing an old sardine box, its long, white beard waving in the wind. John, turning to the conductor, says: "This is one of those cows, ain't it?" "Yes," was the reply. "Well," remarked John, "I think you ought to look after that cow right away, as its milk is spoiling; I could smell it as we passed." The conductor said nothing, though doubtless he felt bad. We soon arrived at the summit of the mountain and found a fine hotel, where we obtained a glass of soda-water—would probably have secured something else, but for the fact that prohibition prevailed in all directions for four miles around. From the hotel three flights of rickety steps take us to the top of the immense rock crowning the summit. As we reach the top of the rock a voice at our elbow says, "Twenty-five cents, please." "What for?" we demand. "This is the charge for visiting the rock," we are informed. We could almost imagine we were in merry old England again, where every one you meet expects you to tip him.

We stopped in Nashville one day and visited Vanderbilt University and the capitol. This is emphatically a Methodist city. The grounds of the University are beautifully shaded with a great variety of native trees, while the air fairly vibrates with the songs of birds. At every turn in the walks is a notice warning visitors against harming or frightening the feathered songsters. We reach St. Louis on the 17th, and have a contest with the railroad officials about our tickets, which had been secured in advance by Mr. Warren Rohr, the agent of the Norfolk and Western road at Lynchburg. We got them properly arranged after a day's hard work and left for Kansas City on the 19th, where we arrived at 8 P. M. and left at 9:40 for this city. As we rolled slowly along the Northern Pacific in our comfortable Pullman car, I noticed in the distance ahead, close to the track, a bright glimmering object, the sunbeams sparkling and flashing from it in beautiful prismatic colors; its round, opaque sides looked familiar, yet for the life of me I could not make out what it was. We approached nearer, and yet nearer, when suddenly it dawned upon me in its full glory. A lone whiskey bottle lay glinting and shimmering in the sun light, all alone and forgotten on the wide prairie. How I longed to hold it in my hands, and perchance to draw the stopper and sniff the faint odor of the departed spirits—of old rye, perhaps, new corn, possibly, of the vile mescal with which I was once familiar, only by sight though, along the Mexican border years ago. Had any other member of the Lynchburg fishing party seen it a mile off they would have recognized it at once; certaily J. K., W. C., G. W. S., E. A. A., or the General would have done so, but as I am noted for my abstemiousness, I may well be excused for my stupidity. Previous to the above incident, I had begun to believe that the prairies held nothing to interest me, and really thought

> "The plain was grassy, wild and bare,
> Wide, wide and open to the air."

Now, however, I discovered that they were, to say the least, not entirely bare.

Touching Denver, a few words at this point. Most of her present leading men came here at the beginning of the town's existence, but their energies were sadly hampered from the fact that everything had to be hauled 600 miles across the plains by teams. It frequently happened that merchants would sell their goods completely out, put up their shutters and go fishing for weeks, before the new semi-yearly supply arrived. Now, with railway communication, all this is changed. She is now a cultivated and beautiful city of 75,000 people. Her streets are very broad, and everywhere shaded with lines of cottonwood trees, abundant in foliage and of graceful proportions. On each side of every street there flows a constant stream of water as clear and as cool as that of a mountain brook, the source of which is a dozen miles southward, whence the water is conducted in an open channel. There are said to be 250 miles of these irrigating ditches and gutters, and 275,000 shade trees. The swish and gurgle and sparkle of waters are always present in Denver, and always must be, for thus she defies the desert and dissipates the dreaded dust. The residents of the city are very proud of their school buildings, which are constructed and managed upon the most improved plans. The fuel of the city was formerly wholly composed of lignite coal which comes from the foot hills, but the extension of the railway to Canyon City, El Moro, and the Gunnison, have made the harder and less sulphurous coal accessible and cheap. The water supply is distributed through forty miles of mains. Average consumption, 3,000,000 gallons daily. There is a paid fire department costing $60,000 annually. A branch of the United States mint is located here. There are eight banks—six national and two State. These facts prove that this city of the desert is upon a firm financial basis. Of the people, it may be said, there is a most charming freedom of acquaintance and intercouse, embellished with the polish and good breeding of rank, devoid of the chill and exclusiveness of regard for "*who was your grandfather.*" Yet this winsome good-fellowship by no means descends to vulgarity or permits itself to be abused.

ON THE RAIL.

Now for the Rockies. Away we go. Why can we not go on always? Have it said of us while living, *going, going;* and, when dead, written over us, gone.

At Denver we take the Denver and Rio Grande railroad, which passes over the most picturesque part of our continent. It is unfortunately a narrow-gauge road, which is its only drawback. The distance it really runs is about 700 miles, which could easily be shortened, to say 550 miles. Inasmuch, however, as it was subsidized by the government in order to secure its construction, it was made as long as possible. For example, say the subsidy was $15,000 a mile, when smooth sections were reached where the road could be built for, say $3,000 per mile, it was made to go over just twice as much ground by curves and twists as was necessary; and thereby $12,000 per mile was secured as profit. All of this is now in process of being looked into by Congress, I believe, and the lands granted are being recovered by the government and opened to settlers.

Our sleeping-car party consists of half a dozen old maids from "Bosting" out on an exclamation pilgrimage, about the same number of young men, and several old gentlemen and their wives. There was one old lady, a widow, going out to California to see her son. This old lady bought a book from a newsboy somewhere near Denver. She lost the book on an average of forty-eight times in every twelve hours. Although she had a comfortable section in the car, she would move her baggage, consisting of a bandbox, a bundle, a bag, a shawl-strap bundle and lunch-basket, from seat to seat all day and every hour in the day, and every time she moved she lost her book "that cost a dollar," the woman informed us at every search. She would break up card parties and tete-a-tete parties every fifteen minutes and have all the baggage piled in the aisles and everybody looking for her book, till she became such a nuisance we all called her by common consent "the old woman with the lost book," and every one in the party commenced to watch her. As soon as she would start on her rounds, some one would say at once, "You put your book in your lunch-basket." She would fish it out and read a few lines, then put it in the bandbox. In a few minutes she would commence looking around, and again would be told where the book was. The old lady finally redeemed herself, however, as will be seen hereafter.

LETTER XI.

THE ROCKY MOUNTAINS—THE GRANDEUR AND SUBLIMITY OF THE SCENERY—AMONG THE MORMONS—SALT LAKE AND SALT LAKE CITY—MEETING OF THE WOMAN OF THE LOST BOOK AND HER SON—ARRIVAL IN SAN FRANCISCO.

ON THE RAIL, July 8, 1888.

My Dear Boy:

We awoke the morning after leaving Denver to find ourselves in the heart of the Rocky Mountains. Our little engine puffs and blows as it drags our train up the slopes and over the high trestles, the canyons in their magnificent grandeur slowly unfolding themselves to view. We pass through the garden of the Gods, with their weird and fantastic rock-capped columns. Everything in view is on a gigantic scale, and, seen from the observation cars, brings forth many exclamations of delight. One characteristic of the Rocky Mountains is its system of vast indentations, cutting through from top to bottom of the range. Some of these take the form of funnels, others are deep, tortuous galleries, known as passes or canyons, but all have their openings toward the plains. A theory: The descending masses of air fall into these funnels or sinuous canals, as they slide down, concentrating themselves and acquiring a vertical motion. When they issue from the mouth of the gorge at the base of the range they are gigantic augers, with a revolution faster than man's cunningest machinery, and a cutting edge of silex obtained from the first sand heat caught up by their fury; thus armed with their own resistless motion and an incisive thread of the hardest mineral, next to the diamond, they sweep on over the plains to excavate, pull down or carve in new forms whatever friable formation lies in their path.

A few remarks from the observation car as it passes through the garden of the Gods, and the canyons around the mountain tops, or glides close to the edge of some stupendous cliff of granite and we look down upon a long thread of silver 1,500 feet below, a river of considerable volume, closed in by walls of basaltic rock, rising sheer 1,500 or 2,000 feet above it. The effect of the appalling depth it is impossible to describe. Can you realize what 2,000 feet means when suspended upon two small rails above this height? I cannot form words to express it. If the most gifted writers acknowledge the impossibility of conveying an adequate idea of the extraordinary appearance of this country when describing it in detail, how can I expect to do it in the few lines that I can devote to it? That it is worth coming all the way from Virginia to see, is saying very little. I might try to compare it with something with which you are familiar, but when there is nothing else in the world like it, what am I to do? Well, amid all of this grandeur, we (John and myself) got very tired of one of the old maids that wore magnifying glasses, exclaiming, "Oh, how grand!" "Oh, how superb!" etc., and "See the lovely light and shadow on the snow" (there was lots of snow all around us). Fortunately, just about the time she was in full swing, and as we greatly feared would turn into an exclamation point, a miserable, long-shanked, saw-legged Kansas grasshopper lazily sailed into view, and to our surprise and delight she exclaimed: "Oh, what a lovely bird! How gracefully he flies! What beautiful plumage! Oh, can any one name it?" "Yes, marm," says John, "it is called the great Rocky Mountain condor; they are very scarce now, as the Modoc Indians are quite fond of their flesh, and have, it is said, almost exterminated the race." A funeral pall fell upon the crowd, and the beautiful scenery was enjoyed in peace for the next hour.

We are rapidly whirled down the slope of the mountain, through the foot-hills and out on the alkali plains of Utah. The burning dust fills our eyes and nose; they are inflamed; our lips crack and seem parched; to laugh is agony, and to move a muscle of the face makes it feel as though we had on a mask tightly glued to the skin. We roll in our berth and awake in Salt Lake City. We are soon out of the cars and among the Mormons. Our first visit is to the new tabernacle, so called to distinguish it from the old tabernacle which formerly stood near it. There is nothing very attractive about the outside appearance of this building; to be appreciated, it must be viewed from the inside. It is elliptical in shape, 250 feet long by 150 wide, and 70 feet high from floor to ceiling. The interior of the building presents an oval arch without any centre supports— the largest self-supporting arch in the United States, I am told. A little south of the tabernacle stands the temple, which is a superb granite building, copied, I think, from a description of Solomon's temple. The following inscription appears on a large tablet stone placed in the face of the east centre tower:

"Holiness to the Lord."
"The House of the Lord."
"Church of Jesus Christ of Latter Day Saints."
"Commenced April 6, 1853."
"Completed ———, ——."

The corner-stone was laid in April, 1853, as stated in the inscription, but it will be many years yet ere this building is completed. About one block away stand the residences of the late Brigham Young. The first is known as the Lion House; a statue of a lion, crouching, being placid over the entrance. The Bee-Hive house comes next; a carved bee-hive (the insignia of Utah) crowns this edifice. Near by are several houses occupied by the deceased Young's wives, among which the most imposing is Amelia's palace. The altitude of the city is more than 4,000 feet above sea level. All of the streets are bordered with shade trees and *running brooks*. Every street is 132 feet wide, so you can well imagine it is a city of "magnificent distances."

About noon we take the cars for Salt Lake, and after a run of fifteen miles reach Lake Park, a popular bathing place. The writer dons a bathing suit and in he goes. The water of the Lake contains 22 per cent. of pure salt, rendering it so buoyant that the least possible effort is necessary to maintain one's epuilibrium. As sinking is out of the question, I float for almost fifteen minutes with feet and hands out of the water. For a long time the wonders of this marvelous salt sea have been heralded afar, but the theme is one of never-ceasing interest, which can be dwelt upon in a thousand moods without risk of tiring the reader. Island mountains spring from its blue depths, whose lonely shores are rarely traversed by human footsteps, and whose heights have never been explored. What wild and romantic scenes, fraught with mystery of isolation and seclusion, may lie hidden amid their lofty summits no one can say. They lie silent and solitary in the wilderness of forbidding waters. There is a place on Church Island where a sharp and rocky ridge stretches down to the sea, where the stormy northwest winds of centuries have hollowed out the rocks along the shore, carving them into fantastic shapes, which point their fingers skyward, or arch gracefully over the green waves that lap against them. On this shore the wild winds fling the spray up the cliffs, coating them with salt that hangs in stalactites in the crevices and on the dead limbs of the stunted trees, or glistens like glass on the smooth, round boulders piled along the coast.

Sea gulls, with snowy plumage, sweep over the crusted water in great numbers. This Dead Sea of America—is there anything on earth like unto it? I cannot believe that the broken walls that now cover the sites of Sodom and Gomorrah can compare with it. We return to the city and take the South Pacific for San Francisco.

Away we rush through the alkali desert again. At Humboldt Sinks we witness the mirage, a seeming lake of sparkling water, which proves to be only a wide plain of alkali. Oh! how our eyes inflame, and smart and sting. Our lips are dry and parched. Water gives but little relief. Our hair and beard feel like wire and our cheeks are seamed and wrinkled like "She" after her second bath in the purple fires of immortality. We draw near the Sierras, and begin to feel the cool mountain breezes.

At a station just as we enter the foot-hills of California, a powerfully built man, apparently about forty-five, enters our car. After a careful scrutiny of each member of our party, he stopped at my seat and asks: "Is there a Mrs. Wade on this car?" "Yes," I say, and point out the old woman with the lost book. A great, joyful light shines in his eye: "Mother, mother! don't you know me? I am Harry!" The old lady attempts to rise—she throws her arms around Harry's neck. "Oh, God, I thank Thee, it is my boy." We are spell-bound; we forget the time, place, everything, and live, move and have our being in Harry and his ma. She laughs and we all laugh.

Our parched lips crack open. Our crisp cheeks split in every direction. We are in agony; she cries—we all cry—she laughs again—we don't laugh any more, but continue to cry and keep it up till the cars roll into Sacramento. " Twenty-five minutes for fresh air," calls out the porter—out we all tumble and drink soda-water and *such like* by the quart. Away we skim over the wide wheat fields of California— past immense orchards of figs, apricots, cherries and peaches, all in full bearing. At the first station out from Sacramento, " Harry " gets out and buys a dozen large figs for his ma. She beams on the dear boy and declares there is nothing she likes half so well as figs; he makes her eat them all. At the next station he buys a dozen large apricots; she eats them all for her dear boy's sake. We all get uneasy. At the next station Harry buys a dozen large plums; he says she must eat them. She says she will try, to please him. She eats two or three; a far-away look comes over her kind, motherly face. She toys with another plum, tries to eat it; then rises suddenly and rapidly retires to the ladies' dressing room and does not return for half an hour. She looks pale, but there is a happy light in her eyes as they dwell fondly on her boy. We all forgive the old lady, and would consider it a privilege to look for her book from now till we reach San Francisco, which we do very soon.

LETTER XII.

SAN FRANCISCO — ITS PERFECT CAR SYSTEM — MARVELOUS FRUITS AND FLOWERS—HORRORS OF THE CHINESE QUARTER—AN OLD VIRGINIA DINNER—OLD FRIENDS—SUTRO PARK, &C.

SAN FRANCISCO, June 8, 1888.

My Dear Boy:

This is a city of enterprise and improvement. The street-car system is the most perfect in every respect that I have ever seen. Although some of the hills are far steeper than Bridge street or even Courthouse Hill in Lynchburg, yet the cars rush up and down them at a rate of seven or eight miles an hour, and withal run so smoothly that you can write comfortably on them. All this is due to the cable system.

The fruits and flowers are marvels of beauty and perfection. Only think of cherries as large as our blue plums, apricots as large as our peaches, with everything in the fruit and vegetable line formed on a corresponding scale. The walks and drives, lined with rose and fuschia bushes, pinks and geraniums, all in great profusion, of mammoth size and wondrous odor, is most enticing to the stranger.

There is one serious blot, however, upon this otherwise lovely picture, which it is well at this point to mention. It comes from the horrible, all-pervading smell of Chinatown. It possesses an individuality that no other odor on earth can lay claim to. On cold, froggy mornings, or at a mild, windy dawn, long before other smells are up, this smell has had its fires made, had breakfast and is ready for business. It hates a " Melican man," and will skip around a corner or jump a dozen blocks to do him an injury. Old travelers have told me that with a favorable breeze you can smell China for fifty-miles out at sea. I doubted this at one time. My doubts have been dispelled since my visit to the Chinese quarter of San Francisco. This portion of the city is an exact counterpart of the towns and cities in the Chinese Empire, and for filth, degradation, immorality and disease, it is doubtful if its counterpart can be found on our continent. I can readily understand, after my few days stay here, why the Pacific coast people are willing to vote for any one, be he *Republican*, *Democrat* or *Devil*, that will relieve them of this curse to progress and to christianity. Even Dr. Hannon informed me of the utter hopelessness of doing anything with this people.

Mr. Marion Langhorne and his charming and hospitable sister, Mrs. Langhorne, gave John, Dr. Hannon and the writer, a regular old Virginia dinner, and seasoned it with true, refined Virginia hospitality. We met Mrs. Langhorne's son, an intelligent, handsome young gentleman of about twenty one years, who is holding a very responsible position in the Pacific steamship service. I am more than ever impressed with an idea that has long been one of my strongest convictions, viz: that it is not worth while to be born at all unless one can be born in old Virginia. An old college-mate and friend of the writer, "Gus" Berlin, attorney-at-law, was exceedingly kind to John and myself during our sojourn. He took us out to the Cliff House, some four miles from the city. From the hotel balcony we could see hundreds of sea lions sunning themselves on the rocks a few hundred feet out in the ocean; their roaring and barking was incessant. Just above the hotel, on a high plateau of several acres in extent, are the most beautifully laid out grounds I ever saw. This is Sutro Park, owned and occupied by Mr. Adolph Sutro, of tunnel fame. From the ramparts of the high wall surrounding this park nothing can present a more sublime and beautiful appearance than the wide, gently rolling waters of the Pacific under an azure sky without a cloud. The eye sweeps over a vast watery plain of the deepest blue, which extends even beyond the ken of the imagination. On our right we see the Golden Gate, through which ocean vessels must needs enter the bay at San Francisco. By the way, this is a veritable land of gold. The conductor of our car coming out had a full set of teeth, upper and lower, of solid gold. Ask John, if you don't believe me.

LETTER XIII.

LEAVING CALIFORNIA—OFF FOR THE SANDWICH ISLANDS—PACIFIC OCEAN MUSINGS—CELEBRATING THE FOURTH—"HOME, SWEET HOME"—A TOUCHING SONG BEAUTIFULLY SUNG.

S. S. MARIPOSA, July 6, 1888.

My Dear Boy :

Promptly at 3 P. M., Sunday, we started out from the Oceanic wharf, and down the bay, and within an hour we passed through the Golden Gate and were on our long journey across the wide Pacific. Looking over the wide waste of waters, my mind reverted to the old Spanish adventurers. I thought of Vasco Nunez de Balboa, the first discoverer of this ocean, who took possession of it in the name and for the benefit of the Spanish Crown in the following high-flown style: "Long live the high and mighty monarch, Don Ferdinand, and Donna Juanna, Sovereigns of Leon and of Arragon, in whose name and for the royal Crown of Castile I take real and corporeal and actual possession of these seas and lands and coasts and ports, and islands of the South and all thereunto annexed," etc., etc., etc.

It was indeed one of the most splendid discoveries that had yet been made in the new world, and must have opened a boundless field of conjecture to the wondering Spaniards. The imagination delights to picture the splendid confusion of their thoughts. Was this the great Indian Ocean, studded with precious islands, abounding in gold and gems and spices, and bordered by the gorgeous cities and wealthy marts of the East, or was it some lonely sea locked up in the embraces of savage, uncultivated continents and never traversed by a bark, save the light pirogue of the Indians? The latter could hardly be true, for the natives had told the Spaniards of golden realms and luxurious and populous nations upon its shores. Perhaps it might be bordered by various peoples, civilized in fact, yet differing from European civilization, who might have peculiar laws and customs, arts and sciences; who, in truth, might form a world of their old, inter-communing through their mighty ocean and carrying on commerce between their own islands and continent, but who might exist in total ignorance and independence of another hemisphere. At the period of which I write, no dream was too wild to entertain, and even at the present time there is a mystery and an enchantment that hangs over this mighty body of water that renders it a constant theme with the novelist.

Among our passengers are T. C. Williams, wife, son and daughter, and Maj. Ginter, niece and servant, of Richmond. Almost as soon as we passed out of the Golden Gate a squall struck us, and almost every passenger became sick; even John, who has crowed over me since our trip to Europe last year, when he proved himself such a good sailor, collapsed completely, and was as sick, yellow and disconsolate a poor fellow as I ever saw. All night the wind howled through the rigging, and our little tub (for she is no better) rolled and tossed. The next day opened calm and bright. We all gathered on deck on the 4th of July and celebrated it in great style. We had two orations. A girl twelve years old repeated the Declaration of Independence; a lot of New Englanders sang the "Star Spangled Banner," and a party of Englishmen sang "God save the Queen." There were toasts and short talks, songs and long sentiments, etc., while altogether we had quite a jolly day.

We have had the trade-winds with us for several days—at least I suppose it is the trade; at any rate, a soft, gentle breeze has filled our sails, yet the waves have been scarcely perceptible. We are bowling along on an almost even keel. All space is filled with a divine gray-blue effulgence, which has to my wondering fancy always seemed to be the trade-wind itself—the only visible wind I know of. It is not too hot nor too cold, not too bright nor too dull; and the ship is going fast and smooth, keeling over just enough to make everything you lean against as pleasant as a rocking-chair, going with a gentle, heaving motion for which it would be absurd to hunt up a simile, because there is nothing so wonderfully delightful wherewith to compare it. There are clouds, slow-sailing clouds, but they are of frosted silver, and there is open sky, but of the very faintest blue, save immediately overhead where the delicate needle of our top-gallant mast sweeps across it in a shortened arc and where it is a faint purple. There are sounds; one a gentle, universal rush, that of wind itself filling space, and others, supplementary voices; the low, gentle lapping of the waves upon the ship's sides and the sleepy, gurgling and hissing of many eddies around her. All things seem to be going one way with some settled purpose. The clouds seem to be leading the wind and the wind to be steadily following the clouds, while the blue and purple waves, a joyous, busy crowd, seem to be hurrying on after both of them to some unknown trysting-place. Yes, I *know* we are in the trades. If the above is not mine, whose is it?

What a lazy, good-for-nothing life we are leading; we rise at 8 A. M. and breakfast; then a short walk of perhaps half an hour; then to our deck chair; luncheon at 1 and dinner at 6; tea at 8 to 9, and then to the social hall for games and music. There is a noted singer aboard, traveling "*incog.*" She sang for us last night " Home, Sweet Home." My heart was full to overflowing; my dear ones came vividly before my mind's eye. How beautifully she sang. Towards the close of each verse the god-like voice went sweeping through airy fields of sound like a lark upon the wing, until it paused aloft in a wild, melancholy minor, and then came gently down like the weary bird dropping, tired, sad with too much joy, to its nest amidst the grass. I retired abruptly to my cabin, to lie awake hour after hour and finally sleep and dream of home, wife, children and friends. Day after day this do-nothing existence goes on, till I think of the following lines, and only wish the poor woman had tried a trip across the Pacific. This was her soliloquy:

> "Here lies a poor woman who always was tired,
> For she lived in a world where too much was required.
> Weep not for me, friends, for I am going
> Where there's no reading or writing or sewing;
> Weep not for me, friends, for when life's thread doth sever,
> I'm going to do nothing for ever and ever."

She could have found no better place on earth to do nothing than on the deck of a Pacific steamer. We expect to sight Honolulu soon, and then for a few hours on *terra firma* and a glimpse of the lands of fruits, flowers, volcanoes, lepers and other queer, horrible, beautiful and wonderful things.

LETTER XIV.

THE SANDWICH ISLANDS—VISIT TO CONSUL SCHAEFER—CHARMINGLY ENTERTAINED—HORRORS OF LEPROSY—BEAUTY OF THE ISLAND OF HONOLULU AND ITS HARBOR—HARROWING STORY OF A WRECK.

HONOLULU, S. I., July 8, 1888.

My Dear Boy :

We arrived in port at 8 A. M. to-day, and in ascending the grand stairway from the saloon to the deck saw the following posted notice: "The Mariposa will sail at 2 P. M., sharp." John and myself promptly disembarked, and securing a carriage, drove to the Hawaiian Hotel, where we breakfasted. Our fruit bill of fare consisted of cantaloupes, mangoes, bananas, figs and a half dozen other tropical fruits with unpronounceable names. Immediately after breakfast we hired a carriage and proceeded to "do the town." We drove to Diamond Head, an extinct volcano which rears its lofty head seven hundred feet above sea level; passed cocoanut and banana groves and cottages embowered in flowers of every hue and in the greatest profusion. During our drive, a cavalcade of native women passed us, riding cavalier fashion and going at top speed. You can imagine our surprise when we learned that there was not a woman's saddle on the island, and that not only the native women, but the white, all ride man fashion. All of the natives, whites and Chinese, wear the native costume called holoku, which is simply our Mother Hubbard, only a little more so. When riding, they put on bloomers under the holoku, and wear a spur on each foot.

At 10:30 we drove up to Mr. Shaefer's to present a letter given the writer by our townsman, Mr. Edmund Schaefer, to his brother, who is German consul here. Had I been searching for the lost garden of Eden I could have rested content here. To say that this is a wondrously beautiful place does not convey the shadow of the substance. Only think of acres of smooth, green grass interspersed with tropical flowers, fruits, cocoanuts, mangoes, mountain apples, bananas, and in fact everything to please the eye or gratify the palate. Just behind the house rises in majestic grandeur a mighty mountain peak, on whose top ever circles a misty cloud, and as we look away down the misty slope—a mile away—there glimmer the ever-varying waters of the parti-colored Pacific, with its foam crested breakers rolling over the coral reefs, which almost completely encircle the island. No brother, no life-long friend could have been kinder to us than were Mr. Shaefer and his charming wife. Everything that kind hearts could do was done for us, and there was no mistaking the genuine hospitality of our entertainers. Even their little ones vied with each other in efforts to make our visit pleasant; and when we left, which was not till

1:30, our carriage was loaded down with tropical fruits, the gift of our new friends. This visit will ever remain an oasis in our memory. Mr. Childs reremarked that there might be many good and beautiful women in Honolulu, but that he felt perfectly satisfied that Mr. Schaefer had drawn the prize of King Kalakaua's domain. 1 say, amen.

This group of islands constitute a perfect paradise, with one exception: the dark cloud that constantly hovers over everything is that most loathsome of all diseases, leprosy. A boat leaves Honolulu for the Leper Island; the heart-rending cries of husband separating from wife, mother and father from their children, and lover from sweetheart, ring in our ears and go echoing up to the great white throne, till my heart asks the question, Why does a merciful God allow this dreadful scourge to afflict his children? Does it doubt the goodness of God? I cannot answer. Such misery I never saw before. This disease is beyond the power of my feeble pencil to describe. It first shows itself in the bleared eyes of the victim, then the fingers and toes drop off joint by joint, the cheek-bones protrude through the flesh and skin, the lobes of the ears elongate—but I will stop; it is too horrible to think or write about. The wife of our chief commissioner spent a year on the Islands, and gave me an account of some of her experiences. During the first three months of her stay she took milk and butter from one of her Hawaiian neighbors. About the close of her third month's residence, a friend asked her who furnished her with milk and butter. She gave the name of the neighbor. "Why, he is a leper," remarked the gentleman (a Catholic priest). "Look at his hand when he brings your supply to-morrow." "I don't believe it," remarked Mrs. McCoppin; "they would send him to the Leper Island." "You will soon learn," the gentleman remarked, "that the natives use every effort to keep the disease from the knowledge of the authorities," which is a sad fact. Even the King and Court will make no effort to eradicate this scourge, and those now being made are due to the unremitting work of the English and American residents. Well, the next morning Mrs. McCoppin received the milk-man in person, and to her dismay found that the joints of his fingers on the left hand were all gone. In a few days the man and one or two members of his family were banished to the Leper Island. She also told me of a woman (native) who married; her husband developed a case of leprosy and was banished to the Island. This is a legal divorce. This woman married again, and within the year the second husband became a leper and was banished. Again she married, and again her husband was a leper in twelve months, yet all this time she had shown no sign of the disease. She went with her third husband to the Island, and to-day she is a leper as white as snow. Mrs. Schaefer informed me that there are three Catholic priests who went to the Island to teach these poor creatures of our Lord, who are to-day loathsome lepers. Does

God require any such sacrifice as this of us? I cannot believe it. But enough of this.

What would I not give to be able to describe the beauty of this Island and harbor! A great billowy waste of mountain lay beyond the town, among which played the shadows of the over hanging clouds at their games of hide-and-seek, graciously merry in the eyes of the happy man, but sadly solemn to him in whose heart the dreary thoughts of the past are engaged at a similar game. Just below the clouds, snowy sea-gulls, not unlike the thoughts of a lady, flitted about in gradually lessening circles until they seemed suspended in the soft air over our heads. The marked variation in the color of the ocean among the coral reefs is magical. Close to shore it is a delicate grey, then a distinct line of bottle green, then pale blue, next orange yellow, and then dark green, and still again the darkest blue tint, with many other magic colors, striking in their effect as viewed beneath the clear evening light and embossed with the rays of the glowing sun. The streets of the Hawaiian capitol are clean and admirably macadamized with coral, lava, stone and sand. At night they are lighted up with electricity. The city has about 30,000 inhabitants. But a brief time has elapsed since this was a wilderness, peopled by a race of cannibals; to-day, nearly all the rising generation can read and write. The government spends $50,000 a year on local schools. The present King, Kalakaua, is very fond of gin and fast horses, yet he is said to be a man of more than ordinary intelligence and a considerable degree of culture. Morally, he has no traits of character which command respect, and is at times so much given to a sensual life as to outrage all kingly associations, incurring the disgust of even his most intimate associates. He is remarkably superstitious, which is indeed a prevailing trait of the entire nation. I was much surprised at the color of the Hawaiians. They are of a very light yellow, in fact some of them brighter than the Chinese, and many of them quite handsome, and all of them graceful in their bearing. Obesity is the highest type of beauty among the natives, and as "poy," which is the national dish, has the effect of fattening rapidly, there are consequently very few natives that are not handsome after the order of their own estimate. The currency of the Island is silver, the denominations of the coins being 10c., 25c., 50c. and $1.00. I saw no gold or notes. United States 5c. nickels are used for small change. I saw no smaller coins.

ON BOARD THE MARIPOSA.

Our steward is quite a character—he has gotten John and myself down quite fine. The first day at table John declined soup. On taking our seats at dinner the second day, the steward remarked to John: "You don't go the soup racket to-day, sir. Will you have some fish?" "No, thank you," says John. "Oh!" says the steward, "you don't take to fish worth a cent, either, sir." When I reach the table I always find a plate of soup, and as soon as it is finished Harry, our steward, says, "Next on bill, I suppose, sir?" I invariably say yes, not that I eat much, as all my friends know, but I go through the bill just to kill time. The eggs on our boat are in a condition that would make Jim Kyle's heart leap for joy. We dare not have them cooked in any other way than that of scrambled. In fact, they won't stand it. *En passant*, you see ducks everywhere on Hawaiia. They are hatched by simply placing the eggs in rice straw, and leaving the straw out in the sun (and moon too) day and night for a week, when out run the little ducks. The mother duck never thinks of setting on them.

Our purser gave me an account of the wreck of the Henry James and the rescue of the crew from Palmira Island on the last trip of the Mariposa from Sydney. There were thirty-five persons, including two women and several children; also one dog. They had been on the Island six weeks, subsisting on crabs, small eels caught with forked sticks among the coral rocks, cocoanuts and young sea birds. Their only cooking utensil was a tin meat-can which held about one-half gallon; in this, cooking was carried on all day long. The vessel was wrecked on a coral reef about thirty-five miles from Palmira Island, and it was so sudden and complete that the crew and passengers had only time to get out two boats and make for the Island, the nearest point from which to get help being the Samoan Islands, 1,400 miles away.

Five of the castaways agreed to take one of the boats and try to make these Islands and bring help for the others. They took seven pounds of the bread (one half of the entire quantity saved from the ship), some eels, crabs, and 250 cocoanuts. When they reached a point near the Samoan Islands, they were all exhausted, but providentially the boat was seen drifting about by a passing ship near the harbor and picked up. The men were all insensible but one, and he was too weak to give any account of himself and his companions until the following day. When this tale was heard, a vessel started to the relief of the poor wretches, but owing to heavy weather returned. About this time the Mariposa arrived on her way to San Francisco, and as soon as her commander, Capt. Hayward, heard of the condition of the unfortunates, he promptly started to their assistance, although it took him out of his course. (I do not admire our captain at all, but am glad to be able to write the above to his credit. With one or two exceptions, I think he has no admirers on the ship, but he is doubtless a safe officer, and this is everything in the "fix" we are in, and 4,000 miles from land.) When the Island was reached, the people were found to be in a horrible condition, almost naked; their skin actually parched like leather, hair matted and offensive odors emanating from the body, &c. They were promptly taken aboard; clothing was given them by the steamer's passengers, which they donned after hot baths and the use of scissors and razor by the barber. When they again made their appearance on deck they did not know each other. One hundred pounds was raised by the passengers and divided among them, and when they reached Honolulu they were placed under the care of the English consul. I hope we may have no such experience on this trip.

This letter will be mailed at Tutuila.

LETTER XV.

OFF FOR AUCKLAND—THE SAMOANS—THEIR LACK OF SUS-
CEPTIBILITY TO IMPROVEMENT—OLD WHALING GROUND
—LEAVING THE TORRID ZONE—VARYING THE MONOT-
ONY OF A LONG VOYAGE

S. S. MARIPOSA,
AT SEA, July 20, 1888.

My Dear Boy:

The Sunday after we left Honolulu—Monday with the Samoans, or Kanakas, as they are called (indeed, the most of the natives of these South Sea Islands are said to be of this latter race; they have the red tinge, first noticed at Honolulu; the same large, dark eyes and long, waving hair and handsome physique). Our experience among them to-day, will long be remembered as a red-letter period in our wanderings.

About eleven o'clock a dim, misty outline of peaks and gently undulating hill-tops could be seen about sixty miles ahead. This, we were informed, was Tutuila, one of the Samoan or Navigator group. As we rapidly approached I could see through my glass a small sailing vessel—the mail boat from Apia—beating up and down, waiting for our steamer, and, on approaching still nearer, I could distinguish six large, long, native canoes loaded down with the red skinned aborigines, so that the water reached almost to the top of the gunwales. They had on a beautiful suit of tattooing, their own long hair, and nothing else. Each boat held about twenty-five men, women and youths. When we had arrived within a mile of the Island our engine stopped, and the boats came on with a rush; each native had a paddle about four feet long, and every one handled it to suit him or herself, without any regard to concert of action with their neighbor. We began to cheer, and the six boats commenced a race, cheering each other to top speed by wild cries. It was a wild, weird-looking sight, their red, oiled bodies glistening under the bright rays of a vertical tropical sun like burnished copper. In a few moments they had thrown their cocoanut-fibre ropes to willing hands and were swarming up the side of the steamer, but just as their boats touched the side of our vessel, those who designed coming on deck donned their breech-cloths. Some of them were put on very hurriedly; the result may safely be left to the imagination of the reader. In a few moments we were engaged in traffic. War-clubs, spears, beads, shells, cocoanuts, fruits, &c., &c., were all and severally offered for $10—"ten dollar"—and bought for a shilling. The natives know no other coin or price, so say $10 whenever asked the price of anything, yet are willing to take a shilling, quarter of a dollar or any piece of money of that size having the appearance of silver; any smaller sized coin they will promptly refuse.

They are a much finer looking people than the Sandwich Islanders. Their features are clear cut, no trace of resemblance to the negro being apparent, and are the merriest looking lot of beggars I ever saw. I have picked up some queer curiosities lately, and among them an entire change of ideas about what is good for the "heathen." We had an addition to our passenger list at this point consisting of a lieutenant from a German man-of-war stationed here; he will go with us to Sydney to spend some time recuperating his health. I learned from him some very interesting facts relative to the natives, their habits, etc. They are very hospitable and kind to all strangers, fairly worshiping the whites, supplying them with everything the Island affords, such as yams, cocoanuts, bread-fruit and all of the tropical fruits and nuts, together with fish and wild hogs, the latter the progeny of those left by Captain Cook. The natives are not fond of meat; cannibalism is not practiced among any of the islands in this group.

On the 16th the air became cool and bracing, suggesting that by the end of the week overcoats would not only be comfortable but absolutely necessary. Flying fish are numerous; they spring from the water at the side of our ship and go skimming over the waves in singles, pairs and in large schools, to great distances. On the 18th the water became very rough, rendering most of us again *actively ill*, myself among the unfortunate number. A few days ago we were sweltering under a tropical sun, listless, lifeless, dripping with perspiration; at night feeling like we were wrapped in a blanket freshly dipped in boiling water. To-day (the 20th) we are all looking blue and pinched, with a freezing south breeze blowing and everybody wrapped up in overcoats and furs. A north wind at home means cold; a north wind here means heat. Yesterday a huge whale came to the surface to breathe, not more than three hundred yards from our vessel, showing a great part of its enormous bulk. This part of the ocean was once the favorite ground for very large fish in years gone by, when whale fishing was profitable. We nightly vary the monotony of this long voyage with concerts, readings, recitations and sleight-of-hand performances. We have on board, bound for the Melbourne Exhibition, a noted magician, who adds greatly to our enjoyment.

We sighted New Zealand about 8 o'clock this morning, and, as I close this letter and at 1 P. M., we are well into the Island, and will probably anchor at 3 P. M. in Auckland.

LETTER XVI.

NEW ZEALAND—INTERESTING FACTS RELATING TO THE MAORIS—A PEST OF RABBITS—THE ALBATROSS—FROM AUCKLAND TO SYDNEY—A DARK AND BREEZY TIME.

AUCKLAND, N. Z , July 25, 1888.

My Dear Boy :

A band just outside my window has been playing "Home, Sweet Home" to welcome the return of a local political favorite from an electioneering tour. A lonely, unheeded stranger was also in hearing under the deep blue canopy studded with stars, whom those familiar strains moved to quickening tears. But we cannot stop our onward march through life to indulge in sentiment. "This world is a bog," said Queen Elizabeth, "over which we must trip lightly. If we pause we sink."

It is not a hundred and twenty-five years since the first landing of Captain Cook in New Zealand, and yet in that comparatively brief period the numerous native population then swarming upon its shores have dwindled to a mere handful. It requires no prophet to foretell that the race will soon be extinct. In Australia many of the native tribes have entirely disappeared—not a single representative being left. The Maoris are far superior to the Australians in appearance and intellect; indeed, are very like our finest type of Indians, yet, like the Indian, they are rapidly giving place to the Anglo-Saxon race. The Maoris are often met in the streets of the cities, dressed in European clothes, and it is very amusing to see them salute each other, which they do by rubbing their noses together. The men tatoo themselves all over the face, the women only about the chin and mouth. I did not find these people a cleanly race; those that occupy the Hot Lake district are said to spend two-thirds of their time in the water, and are doubtless less dirty. The full-bloods are a fairly good looking race, but the half-breeds are remarkably handsome. Like our Indians, they make the women do all the drudgery; the men hunt and fish. It seems strange that while these people were cannibals they throve and increased, but since civilization has been introduced there has come annual decimation. There is one feature seen in every Maori's face which is marvelously beautiful, viz.: the eyes; they are large, black as night and brilliant, full of feeling and tenderness. The Maoris as a race have some striking peculiarities. For example, they never eat salt; they have no fixed industry, and no idea of time of its divisions into hours and months. They are like our Indians, constitutionally lazy; they are intensely selfish, and care nothing for their dead. They have a quick sense of insult, but cannot, as a rule, be called pugnacious; they excite themselves to the fighting point by indulging in a hideous war-dance and singing songs full of braggadocio, and when thus wrought up they are perfectly reckless as to personal safety. He is not, however, a treacherous enemy; he gives honorable notice of his hostile intent, warring only in an open manner, thus exhibiting a degree of chivalry unknown among our Indians. Money with them is considered only as representing so much tobacco and whiskey, or rum. Alcohol is their criterion of value—bread and meat are quite secondary. "White man drink whiskey, why not I," says the Maori; they will beg for drink, but not for bread. Those that know them best say it is quite impossible to imbue them with a sense of the importance of chastity; the idea is altogether ignored. But after a woman is married she becomes sacred, and to treat her with unchaste violence then, is to incur the penalty of death. It would be impossible to imagine a more immoral people than the Maoris, judging by our standards.

Ancient traditions are fast dying away among these people—dying with the elders of their tribes, in whose memories they are locked up. The missionaries half invented, half transcribed an oral Maori language, which was used to translate the Bible. But there cannot be said to exist any native literature. The aborigines gave themselves the name Maori—pronounced Mau-re. We are told by well-informed writers upon this subject, that they were of all the South-Sea tribes the most intelligent. They are physically the most vigorous of any savages inhabiting islands south of the equator. Wherever they are now found in the neighborhood of cities, they usually adopt European clothing, yet we are told amusing anecdotes of their going back into the "bush" from time to time, solely to indulge in the old savage condition of nudity, and to enjoy a sense of entire freedom from the conventionalities of the whites. There is not much inter-marriage between the whites and natives now, but when there were few white women it was not so uncommon. The race evinces to-day many of the wild traits of their ancestors. You cannot quite tame an Apache, a Gypsy, or a New Zealand Maori. Polygamy and slavery still exists among them. They believe in a future state of existence, and build rude temples to a great spirit, but as late as 1840 their greatest delight was the war-dance, the cannibal feast and the boasting war-song. The Maori affords us the anomaly of a braggart who is not by any means a coward. Now and then is seen among them a face of unmistakable Jewish cast, which sets the imagination to work to find some possible connection, far back among bygone ages, between this race and the Hebrew.

The Maoris, when first discovered, had many games and sports which were identical with our own, such as kite-flying, skipping-rope, hide-and-seek, dancing, walking upon stilts, &c. Cook estimated, when he first visited them, they had passed the period of their best days. He thought that in the century previous to his coming, they had eaten about one-fourth their number. The race now numbers about 35,000, though it is certain it aggregated over 100,000 a century ago. The half-caste seldom lives to be over forty years—of the pure blood you will see but few old persons. They are all, both men, women and children, most inveterate smokers. What a blessing it would be to old Virginia if there were 35,000,000 of them instead of 35,000. You can give a Maori nothing more acceptable than a pipe and a plug of tobacco. When a Maori meets another after a long separation, the first thing is a mutual rubbing of noses, after which each of the parties begins to weep and moan, but when they say good-bye, be it in view of never so long a separation, they indulge in the most boisterous laughter. As the dead lie prepared for burial, the nearest of kin first, then the closest friends, rub noses with the corpse.

The Maoris live nearly like the lower class of animals, preferring that sort of life even after half a century of intercourse with the whites. They may, from motives of policy, listen to and pretend to accept christianity, as many of the Chinese do; but *both races*, it is well understood, return to their original faith at the first opportunity. The modern Maori accepts the creed of the missionary because it is the easiest thing for him to do, but he still believes in witchcraft, the evil eye, etc. The Roman Catholic faith, which addresses itself so palpably to the eye through form and ceremony, is the most popular among them, and has by far the largest number of professed adherents of any denomination. The decrease in the portion of the Island set aside for them is as rapid as it is where they are brought into more close connection with the whites. As a people, they have manifestly fulfilled the purpose for which God placed them in these Islands of the South Sea, and, like the "Moa," they must pass off the scene and give place to another race of beings. So it is with the Indian, and so it was with the now totally-extinct natives of Tasmania. Nothing can prevent the inevitable. It is *Kismet*.

I have endeavored to be as clear and succinct as possible in this somewhat extended description of an interesting race, and acknowledge my indebtedness to M. M. Ballou's book, "Under the Southern Cross," for aid in writing it. During my short stay among these people I have seen and heard many things that will constitute delightful reminiscences in future days. These are some of their unique names: "Wirernu Turei," "Te Kepa," "Terurahuihui," "Ropata Wohawaha."

In New Zealand rabbits are so abundant that they are killed, skinned, and the carcasses left on the ground to be devoured by carrion birds. The head is always saved and turned into the government for the bounty which is paid upon each one. The skins are packed and shipped to Europe, to be made into gloves, etc. The total claims made to the rabbit branch of the Sydney Land Department for rabbits destroyed amounts to date to £191,351, say $1,000,-000. Mr. Ballou, in his graphic description of this

Island, says: "I have seen, by moonlight, a whole sloping hill-side which seemed to be moving, so completely was it covered by these little furry quadrupeds." They are shot, poisoned, trapped and killed with clubs, but still so rapidly do they breed there is no visible diminution of their number.

The rivers of New Zealand are generally destitute of fish, and the forests and plains of game. It is no country for a sportsman. Vegetation runs riot, however, the soil being very fertile, and drouth is unknown. In this respect it is entirely unlike Australia. In the northern portion it is very much like Spain in climate, the middle not unlike France, while the southern portion is very similar to that of England. At the Christ Church Museum can be seen the skeleton of that most remarkable pre-historic bird, the "Moa." This bird was indigenous in New Zealand, and is supposed to have existed up to a period of 2,000 years ago, probably disappearing before any human beings came to the Island, as the Maori people can only be traced back for some 700 years, and are believed to have come from the Sandwich Islands. Tradition fails to give any account of the gigantic bird "Moa" while living, but their bones are often found in caves, from which the specimens extant have been reconstructed. The head of one of these skeletons stands sixteen feet from the ground, the various portions of the body harmonizing with the height. When standing erect it was several feet higher than the giraffe, and was to the rest of the bird-tribe what our townsman Ike U—— is to a toddling infant.

From Auckland, where this letter was begun, to Sydney, where it will be completed, the sea is always rough, and it certainly did not depart from the prevailing rule to accommodate us. Almost as soon as we steamed out of Auckland the storm was upon us. As night came on it increased in intensity. On we drove through darkness so dense that nothing could be seen fifty feet from the ship. Our lady passengers clung to the arms of their seats in the saloon, and with blanched faces and bated breath, whispered their fears to their male protectors. Those who had heretofore escaped sea-sickness succumbed to this dismal disorder, and were "actively ill." "He that will learn to pray, let him go to sea," says George Herbert. "God maketh the sea to boil like a pot," can be literally understood by any one that has ever crossed it between the two places indicated.

Many an otherwise weary hour was pleasantly passed watching the graceful flight of the albatross, that fateful bird of nautical romance. The ease and apparent lack of effort with which it sustains itself in the air is simply wonderful. What secret power is it that can propel him for hundreds of yards against the wind, with no perceptible motion of the wings? The albatross is armed with the most powerful beak attached to any of the feathered tribe, being from seven to nine inches long, the end of which is a keen, pointed hook as hard as steel. The average size of the bird is: length of body, three feet; spread of wings from tip to tip, ten feet. In many instances the wings will measure twelve feet from tip to tip. The feet are large, say eight inches across, webbed and armed with three sharp claws over an inch in length. The prevailing color is that of a dirty white or dove on the upper part of the body and wings; the breast and under part of the wings are always snowy white. The flight of these birds is so rapid that it is said they could sup at the Cape of Good Hope and breakfast at New York.

We have just arrived (July 26th) at Sydney, after a troubled voyage, and leave this P. M. for Melbourne.

LETTER XVII.

THE MELBOURNE EXPOSITION—THE OPENING CEREMONIES—CHIEF COMMISSIONER AND MRS. M'COPPIN—MEETING NOTABLE PEOPLE.

MELBOURNE, Aug. 6, 1888.

My Dear Boy:

The great Melbourne Exposition opened on the 1st in due form. The high and mighty dignitaries of the world occupied the dais in the centre of the main building. At 11:30 A. M., Sir Henry Loch and Lady Loch entered at the main entrance of the Avenue of the Nations; the various representatives of all the nations on earth marched down the long gallery to receive and escort them to a raised platform. As they passed the various courts, bands of music played national airs, the immense organ in the west nave poured out its powerful tones, the tens of thousands of spectators rose to their feet, and the opening ceremonies had commenced.

Among the supporting escort, one of the most conspicuous, dignified and commanding figures was our chief commissioner, Hon. Frank McCoppin. No title was necessary to inform the spectators that here walked a true gentleman and a man among men. Six feet, four inches in height; straight as an arrow; thoroughly proportioned; complexion ruddy; a short, thick, gray moustache; hair perfectly white, and an eye that took in everything and everybody at a glance. I felt a sincere pride in my countryman, nor can I refrain from saying a word or two in praise of his charming wife. Mrs. McCoppin is just such a woman as Beaconsfield would have taken for one of his characters—a woman with a kind, sympathetic heart, a mind of extraordinary capacity stored with an amount of information simply wonderful, and possessed with the faculty of imparting it in the simplest and most pleasant way imaginable. Her reading extends over the greatest variety of subjects. Politics are quite as familiar to her as are the best poets, while every fiction of any note from Fielding and Smollett to Amelia Rives are entirely familiar to her. Mrs. McCoppin is stout, with a handsome, striking face, and is about forty-five years of age. Among the wealth, beauty and nobility occupying the main stand, there were no two figures more striking than that of our chief and his accomplished wife.

The position of the four assistant commissioners was quite near the principal stand, and a little to the left of the choir of one thousand voices. Miss Sherwood sang a solo, and although the building in which the ceremonies were held is over five acres in floor extent, the main building alone being used, her powerful voice could be heard in every nook and corner. I am quartered just across the street from the Exhibition building; have a small room, and pay four guineas or $20 per week for it and board. I have made numerous efforts to settle down to business and letter writing, but owing to calls from American exhibitors, find it an exceedingly difficult thing to do. I have had the pleasure of meeting Lady Musgrove, daughter of David Dudley Field, and niece of Associate Justice Field of the U. S. Supreme Court, and found her a genuine American in both accent and bearing. You know it is said an Englishman loves a lord above all things. The Australian would give his life almost for a nod from one. Titles are simply adored out here. I have been very kindly treated by every one I have met, and should, and do, feel very grateful, but I would prefer my modest cottage in old Lynchburg to the finest palace in this country.

LETTER XVIII.

AUSTRALIAN FORESTS—THEIR UTTER DESOLATION—HUNTING BEARS AND KANGAROOS—THE RESULT—LAUGHING JACKASSES—THE ART GALLERIES AT THE EXHIBITION—THE DRAMA.

United States Court,
Exhibition Building,
October 3, 1888.

My Dear Boy:

Messrs. Faulkner and Craighill, of Lynchburg, gave me a letter of introduction to a friend of theirs in Melbourne. I was delighted to find that he is as much devoted to sport as myself, and we at once arranged for a hunt for the fol'owing Tuesday. So on that day, accompanied by this friend, we took the train for Goldburn, New South Wales, which was reached Wednesday at 8 A. M. We hired a two-horse trap, and within one hour after our arrival were on our way to "Bungonia," a station in the heart of the colony. We were on the road almost all day. After leaving Goldburn, we entered the forest, which extended for hundreds of miles in every direction.

A word here anent Australian forests. Every square acre is just like every other square acre throughout the whole country. There is no more desolate sight than is presented by these forests. The trees are gnarled and twisted, and all of the trunks and limbs are white, with that peculiar ashy appearance seen only in a pile of bleached bones on some wind-swept desert. The ground underneath the trees is almost entirely bare, as there is but little to fertilize it, the trees never shedding their leaves, but only their dry, sapless, lifeless bark, which peels off in long strips, and lies along the ground in tangled masses. No sound is heard among the trees, except occasionally the peculiar guttural note of the magpie or the shrill pipe of the "soldier bird." I have wandered for hours through these "*skeleton woods*" without hearing even a leaf stir, and only occasionally catching a glimpse of a kangaroo or wallaby scudding away in the distance like a brown shadow. I can now readily understand why the bushmen, when lost in these miles of desolate, white timber trees, with their funereal plumes of "black-green foliage," go mad in a few days, and when found, which seldom happens, are raving maniacs. To a stranger, there is no way of locating one's route of return by any peculiarity of trees or ground, as it is all so exactly alike that only those raised amid such surroundings can navigate through these pathless wastes with anything like safety.

Now for the hunt: I saw my first ferocious Australian bear a few miles from our starting point. He was resting comfortably in the fork of a blue gum, and looked at me as I approached the trees with an air that said, "Well, what do you want here?" I planted a 44-Winchester ball in his back, which only made him move up the trunk of the tree a few feet and commence to cry. The tears streamed down his face, and the cry was so like that of a child in deep distress that my heart reproved me, and I promptly put a ball through its head. I had killed my first bear. During the day we killed twenty-seven bears. We spent three days and a-half in our hunt, killing ninety-two bears, seventy one kangaroo and wallaby, six hares, and parrots innumerable. The most amusing incident of the trip I note here. I was placed on a stand to shoot kangaroo, and the drivers, a squad of six boys, on horseback, were sent to the woods a half mile to drive the poor brutes toward me by " cooing " (Australian for yelling) and cracking whips, though my stand I was told to keep perfectly quiet. Soon after my guide left me I heard some one laugh—the sound seemed to come from the direction of a " water hole " I had passed about one hundred yards in rear of my stand; " ha, ha, ha," then " he, he, he," quickly followed by " ho, ho, ho," and again " hey, hey, hey," then altogether the entire party broke out in the most uproarious, jolly laugh I ever heard, and although I was furiously angry I could not, for my life, keep from joining in it. Knowing that this infernal racket would prevent any sensible animal from coming within a mile of me, I went down to the water hole to request the party to leave, as they were interfering with my sport. When I reached the place no one could be seen. I looked in every direction, and the only thing I saw was five large birds that looked like "king-fishers" on a big scale. Just as I was about to return to my stand completely mystified, I heard " ha, ha, ha," and to my surprise it came from one of the birds; the next one took it up, "he, he, he," and so on, and then altogether in a chorus—the most rollicking, jolly peals of laughter I ever heard. I laid down on the dead grass and rolled over in convulsions, and was only brought to my senses by an "old man" kangaroo jumping almost over me. I picked up my gun and gave him a parting shot, and almost immediately heard my drivers shouting their coo, coo, coo, in the woods near me. I was soon joined by my guide, who informed me that the birds that had amused and annoyed me so much were "laughing jackasses." I met these unique fowls several times afterwards, and had many hearty laughs with them.

I am again hard at work on my tobacco report—subject: tobacco—its growth, progress, etc., having been assigned to me by the commissioner. Almost every night I spend an hour or two in the picture gallery in the Exhibition Building. I am greatly pleased with the German Art Gallery, and will mention a few pictures that have particularly taken my fancy.

"The Only Friend," a fine picture by Hillah, represents a dog lying outside the barred window of a prison, while the inmate has pushed his hand through the iron railings to allow it to rest caressingly on the animal's head. "A Summer Morning on the Beach," by Leistikow, a delicately-toned sea picture, with early summer light lighting up the boats and planks on the sea-shore. "The Norwegian Harbor," by Garebe, and the "Norwegian Fiord" by the same artist. In both, the main feature is the lustrous and pellucid blue of the water, which in the middle distance has caught the tints from the mountains as they rise abruptly from the sides of the narrow bay. "The Sattenfiord," a very glowing composition, with sunlit rocks and shipping, almost dazzling in their warmth of color, is a fine picture. I do not now recall the artist's name. "A Winter Evening," by Muller-Kurzwellz, in which the treatment of sunshine on snow is very realistic, the last gleam falling on the branches of the trees like a thread of gold, and catching the surface of a tiny pool where two aquatic birds are resting. A charming picture is the one entitled "A Moonlight Night," by Schleich, with the moon rising over a gloomy marsh. "Poppies," a richly-painted cluster of leaves and flowers by Mary Bross, is another very fine painting. "The Evening Bell," by Leisklow, represents a landscape fading away into the gray tints of twilight, while a boat is slowly making its way through the rippling water. "Scene Outside an Osteria," in Albino, by Ravenstein — a masterpiece of brilliant coloring — with a bevy of peasant girls dancing to the music which a group of rustic musicians are making. "Autumn Evening" is merely a corner in a forest, glorified by the setting sun, whose reflected rays are bringing out the tints of the surrounding foliage, rocks and branches.

From the French Gallery I will only mention two pictures that made a deep impression upon me. One is a superb painting by Rixens: an angel clasping a dead musician and holding aloft a crown of laurel leaves, while the music sheets have fallen forever from the nerveless hand. The subject is treated with great power. The other picture, entitled "Normandy Pastures," by Barillot, I regard as one of the best animal studies in the Exhibition. The distinctive characteristic of this picture is the brilliant atmospheric tint which lights up the whole canvas and gains its full measure of effect in the soft shadow on the ground.

But enough of pictures. I only look at a few each evening, and will venture a word of advice to my Lynchburg friends, which is founded upon actual experience. Don't go on looking at a succession of pictures until your eyes are pained by the strain upon them, and the faculties of observation, comparison and criticism are wearied, but on the other hand, study a few attentively, until you have mastered their subject, sentiment, spirit and style—all they express and all they suggest, until an *accurate and enduring image* of them has impressed itself upon the tablets of your memory. This is the way to enjoy them prospectively, as well as in the immediate present. When visiting the celebrated galleries of

Europe remember this, and you will find my advice worthy of consideration.

Now for a little city news, and I am done. The good ship "Gaiety," in which Melbourne people have been pleasantly voyaging for the past few weeks, has drifted into a quiet haven, and all on board are now anxious for the rest that a brief respite from merry-making will afford. In fact, society has been so gorged with *fetes* of pleasure during the present month that, were any other brilliant entertainments now organized, the promoters would risk the chance of being socially "boycotted." In the present phase of welcome quietude, afternoon teas, small dinners and theatre parties are the most *excessive* forms of pleasurable dissipation, where little exertion is necessary, and the yield of enjoyment is most satisfactory. Afternoon teas at the Exhibition have become a most popular institution, and during the past week many ladies have played the hostess at these dainty entertainments within the monster show. The theatre parties are receiving due attention, as the dress circles of the Princess and the Bijou theaters nightly attest. At the Bijou on Friday evening, amongst the large audience there were none who so thoroughly enjoyed the drolleries of "The Magistrate" as the ladies in the dress circle.

Miss Essie Jenyns, a native Australian, has gained quite an enviable reputation as an actress. She will leave for England in a few weeks, and will doubtless favor the States, and possibly Lynchburg, with her presence before her return home. There was an overflowing and most enthusiastic audience at the Princess last Saturday evening when she appeared as Rosalind. In the last scene she wore a model gown (Australian for dress) of soft, white material, long train and wide sleeves lined with crimson velvet. On her head was a pearl coronet, and diamond ornaments completed an outfit in which Miss Jenyns looked quite lovely. Lady Loch and the Governor, Sir Henry Loch, who omit no opportunity of evincing their interest in Miss Jenyns, accompanied the vice-regal party to the Princess to-night, when the lovely actress—by special vice-regal command—portrayed the charming wiles and ways of Parthenia, the Greek maiden. My friends must not regard me as stage-struck, or longing for a closer intimacy with colonial nobility. I merely chanced to feel in this vein, hence the above, which may amuse if it does not instruct.

I find the life of a United States commissioner very pleasant, and my path made very smooth and comfortable, yet my heart longs for the clasp of a true friend's hand—

"I sigh for the touch of a distant hand and the sound of a
  voice that is still."

LETTER XIX.

THOUGHTS OF HOME AND FRIENDS—THE ADVANTAGES OF TRAVEL—THE EXHIBITION BUILDING—JAMES WASHINGTON—AN INCORRIGIBLE BACHELOR—SOME REFLECTIONS ON THE RELATIONS BETWEEN AUSTRALIA AND THE UNITED STATES.

MELBOURNE, Oct. 3, 1888.

My Dear Boy:

As the period approaches to turn our faces homeward, memories of that home come thronging thick and fast upon us. How often during the last few days have these lines occurred to me:

> "How brightly gleams the orb of day
>   Across the trackless sea;
> How lightly dance the waves that play
>   Like dolphins on our lee.
> The restless waters seem to say,
>   In smothered tones to me,
> How many thousand miles away
>   My native land must be.
>
> "Speak, ocean! is my home the same?
>   Now all is new to me—
> The tropic sky's resplendent flame,
>   The vast expanse of sea.
> Does all around her, yet unchanged,
>   The well-known aspect wear?
> Oh, can the leagues that I have ranged
>   Have made no difference there?"

How often have I asked myself the question: Is my

home the same? Will I soon clasp the hand and look into the eyes of all the dear friends I left behind? One dear friend I know is gone; than whom no truer, better friend ever lived than Tom Kyle! Will I miss others on my return? God grant it may not be so. This dread of not finding our dear ones on our return is the one great obstacle to the pleasure of travel. That travel enlarges the mind, produces clear-sightedness, tolerance and sympathy, and tends to refine the manners, we must all admit. One thing, however, must be borne in mind relative to travel, wherever it is indulged in. If it is to be productive of lasting good, the traveler must have something to put into his traveling in order that he may get something out of it. There are travelers who have eyes, but they see not, and ears, but they fail to hear and understand; for such persons travel can do but little. Travel is one only of the valuable aids to culture, which includes also reading, reflection, discussion and conversation. It is well to remember that without the others, the teachings of travel will not be very efficacious, and that it is of importance, not only that people should travel, but that it would be always best that they should be such persons as would likely be benefited thereby.

Touching the Exhibition Building, of which I have heretofore said but little or nothing, I will give you a few items about the American court therein. The commissioner's office is a handsome room, situated about midway of the main aisle, at the front door of which stood a tall, strongly-built negro, as black as midnight, his dark uniform, elaborately trimmed with gold lace, only serving to intensify his ebony hue. James Washington is his name, and I believe he attracts more attention than any exhibit we have. There are two assistants, also dressed in blue and gold; they are mulattoes, and all three came from the States. Washington is about sixty years old, and worth, I am informed, $100,000 in property. I asked him if he was married. "No, sir; I gits trouble enough, 'dout havin' no wife." "Don't you know if you marry and have lots of trouble you will be admitted in Paradise when you die, as you will have had all of your allotment on this earth?" "Well," said James, 'Dat's a new doctrine to me, Mr. Miller, but if I knowed it was true I would ruder take my chances in de nex world dan de certainty what I would hab in dis." I then told James Washington it was a Hindoo doctrine, and as some of our Lynchburg friends are unacquainted with the theory, I give them the story as illustrated in verse:

> A Hindoo died—a blessed thing to do
> When twenty years united to a shrew.
> Released, he hopefully for entrance cries
> Before the gates of Brahma's paradise.
> "Hast been through purgatory?" Brahma said.
> "I have been married"—and he hung his head.
> "Come in, come in, and welcome too, my son!
> Marriage and purgatory are as one."
> In bliss extreme he entered heaven's door,
> And knew the peace he ne'er had known before.

He scarce had entered in the garden fair,
Another Hindoo asked admission there.
The self-same question Brahma asked again:
"Hast been through purgatory?" "No—what then!"
"Thou cans't not enter!" did the God reply.
"He who went in was there no more than I."
"All that is true, *but he has married been*,
And so on earth has suffered for all sin."
"Married? 'Tis well, for I've been married twice!"
"Begone! We'll have no fools in Paradise!"

Well, I started to say something about the Exposition, and instead skipped over to India.

There ought to be a feeling of peculiar sympathy on the part of the United States of America towards the Australian colonies on the occasion of those colonies celebrating their centenary. The sympathetic feeling on the part of the United States towards Australia ought to be a vital emotion, because both countries are engaged in the same grand work—that of rearing the human race under conditions such as have never before been known in the history of this planet—under the absolute liberty of the people and their freedom from the oppressions of governing classes who, in less happily circumstanced countries, have so often plunged the people into wars of aggression, and more securely bound the chains of military authority around them at the very time their victims supposed themselves to be patriotically fighting for their country's freedom, or at least for their national aggrandizement. When an enlightened people have the government in their own hands there is little fear of long-continued war ; not only so, but one of the greatest benefits that is found to be growing with the free institutions of the young nations of the United States and of Australia is that of educational enlightenment. The United States is the only country ever known in the history of the world that has spent, and is spending, more money in education than on armaments, and consequently there is reason for hope that the people will in the future increase the national wisdom, and by means of general education may, in the language of Lord Brougham, be " Easy to lead, but hard to drive ; easy to govern, but impossible to enslave."

While in these colonies, as in the United States, the people are learning to appreciate their privileges, to maintain their rights, and, in fact, to carry out the ideal theory of governing, so as to afford the greatest happiness to the greatest number, they are at the same time making a progress in the industrial arts and manufactures that is simply unparalleled in history. One of the advantages which result from free institutions and political equality is, that every man, no matter what country may have given him birth, no matter what his origin may have been, nor what his color is, or his creed may be, has an opportunity to make a living and enjoy it in comparative comfort, happiness, and independence, and has a still higher opportunity by the exercise of honest industry, commercial talent or political ability to become a leader amongst his fellows. The experience of the United

States shows that such freedom and equality are wonderful incentives to that energetic enterprise which means progress, and which has shown in the nineteenth century how such a nation can almost spring into existence. The energy and enterprise referred to are among the most admirable results of the government of the United States, though it is possible that it does not arise solely from the liberal constitution of the country, but also from the additional fact that the people of the United States are, as a nation, necessarily enterprising.

Under the circumstances—that it is the example of progress set by the United States that Australia must follow—it is a matter for regret that the representation of that great country at the Australian Centennial Exhibition is not more complete. What one can see at the Exhibition does not give anything like an adequate idea of the importance of American manufactures. But, as one of its commissioners truly remarked, the United States are well represented in these colonies altogether outside of the Exhibition, and with some great ideas. A visitor may go down from his apartment at his hotel in an American elevator. He will travel to the Exhibition in an American cable tram car. He will pass into the building through an American patent turn-stile, and he will see the place lighted with electric lights, which an American has largely assisted in perfecting. Such appliances as sewing machines and reapers and binders, which are generally used throughout the country, are certainly American in their origin, and there are numerous similar ideas in frequent use which came from that country.

LETTER XX.

ADIEU TO AUSTRALIA—WHERE THE ORIENT AND OCCIDENT MEET—IMPRESSIONS OF THE COUNTRY—THE ACME OF DESOLATION—THE MAORIS—NEW ZEALAND AND SAMOA—MY CHIEF'S HEAD—GENIAL OFFICERS, ETC.

S. S. "ALAMEDA,"
SOUTHERN PACIFIC OCEAN, Oct., 1884.

My Dear Boy:

This letter is begun at Sydney, N. S. W.; just where it will be completed remains for the future to determine. As I am leaving Australia, perhaps forever, my impressions of the country may not be inappropriate in this place. What is the dominant characteristic of Australian scenery? is a natural enquiry that may be very summarily answered as being identical with the dominant character of our own Edgar Allen Poe's poetry, viz: "Weird melancholy." The Australian mountain forests are funereal, secret, stern; their solitude is the perfection of desolation. They seem to stifle in the black gorges a story of sullen despair. No tender sentiment is nourished in their shades. In other lands the dying year is mourned; the falling leaves drop lightly on his bier. In the Australian forests no leaves fall; the savage winds shout among the rock clefts. From the melancholy gum, strips of white bark hang grotesquely or ghostly. Great grey kangaroos hop noiselessly over the coarse grass. Flocks of white cockatoos stream out, shrieking like evil spirits. The sun suddenly sinks and the mopokes burst out into horrible peals of semi-human laughter. From a corner of the silent forest rises a dismal chant, and around the fire dance natives painted like skeletons. All is fear-inspiring and gloomy. Australia has been rightly named the "Land of the Dawning." Wrapped in the midst of an early morning their history looms up vague and gigantic. The lonely horseman riding between the moonlight and the day sees vast shadows creeping across the shelterless and silent plains; hears strange noises in the primeval forest, where flourishes a vegetation long dead in other lands. There is a poem in every tree and flower, but the poetry which lives in the trees and flowers of Australia differs from that of other countries, and makes the observer feel that the trim utilization that bred him, is but an insignificant atom in contrast with the grandeur of these forests that are coeval with civilization itself. Europe is the home of knightly song and gallant deeds. Asia sinks beneath the weighty recollection of her past grandeur as the "Sattee" sinks, jewel burdened, upon the corpse of dead magnificence, distinctive even in its death. America swiftly hurries on her way, rapid, glittering, insatiable even as one of her own gigantic waterfalls. From the jungles of Africa, and the creeper-tangled groves of the South Pacific islands, arise from the hearts of a thousand flowers heavy and intoxicating odors, the upas poison which dwells in barbaric sensuality.

In Australia, alone, is to be found the grotesque, the weird, the strange scribbling of nature learning how to write. Strangers see no beauty in the trees without shade, flowers without perfume, birds that cannot fly and beasts who have not yet learned to walk on all fours. But the dwellers in this strange country acknowledge the subtle charm of this fantastic land of monstrosities; they become accustomed to the beauty of loneliness whispered to by the myriad tongues of the wilderness; he hears the language of the barren and the uncouth, and can read the hyeroglyphics of haggard gum-trees, blown into odd shapes, distorted with fierce, hot winds, or cramped with cold nights, when the Southern Cross freezes in a cloudless sky of icy blue. The phantasmagoria of that wild dreamland, termed "the bush," interprets itself, and the poet of its desolation can well comprehend why free Esau loved his heritage of desert sand better than all the bountiful richness of Egypt.

Now that we are at Auckland, in New Zealand, a few additional words about the Maoris may not be out of place. From all I can learn they would be glad to throw off the English yoke. There is a reservation on the North Island called the "King's Country," where the great bulk of the natives are settled, and into which no white man can enter without permission of the head chief. Yet, strange to relate, the Mormon from Utah has been, and is yet, among these people, and now has a following of more than 3,000. At one time these Mormons seriously contemplated leaving their country to settle among the Mormons in Utah. They were doubtless actuated, in great measure, by their hatred of the English. They are a very intelligent people, considering their opportunities, these Maoris; and did they not plainly see the futility of the effort, they would declare war and attempt the wresting of their island home from the clutch of the invader. Many years ago, when at war with the English, the missionaries were warned to leave. One of them declined to go and was killed. The body was laid on the ground in front of the Mission house and Chief Keropa collected the tribes around it, and as is their custom as also their greatest delight, harangued them, speaking with great contempt of the English. Suddenly, in the midst of his most telling abuse of the enemy, he stooped over the body of the murdered preacher, gouged out both of the eyes and ate them, saying, "Now we can whip the Pakehas." The latter is a name given by the Maoris to all English-speaking people.

We to day passed Sunday Island, which lies about midway between New Zealand and Samoa, and which has a very curious history. The island is about three miles wide by seven long. Many years ago a few Americans left Samoa and settled on this island. They made attractive homes and gathered fine crops from the fertile soil. Occasionally a whaling fleet would visit them, bringing news from the outside world and buying their surplus crops, etc. Ten or twelve years passed, when one day a trading vessel, plying between China and Peru, stopped at the island and sent ashore several boat loads of coolies and sailed away. The horror of the poor islanders can be imagined when they found that the new comers were, without an exception, suffering from small-pox. In a short time every living soul had the disease. Every Chinaman died, and only two or three whites were left alive. These were taken by a passing vessel to Samoa, and for years the island was uninhabited. The next settlers were Americans from Tutuila. They had just gotten settled when a volcanic eruption frightened them off. Next came the present occupant, an American named Bell. His family consists of a wife and eight or nine children, most of them grown. Twelve or fourteen years ago, Bell and his wife decided to take possession of the island, and lead a sort of Swiss-Family-Robinson-Crusoe life. As their children grew, and others were born, the area of cultivation was gradually extended. They have never evinced any desire to leave their island home. A few years ago they petitioned our government to attach it to the United States, and wrote several times to the consul at Auckland, N. Z., urging their request. The policy of our government being adverse to acquiring more territory, Bell failed in his effort. But Great Britain, as we all know, has a very decided talent for acquiring every little speck of land anywhere and everywhere she can, so New Zealand was instructed to gobble up poor Bell's island, which she very promptly proceeded to do. They marked off a paltry five hundred acres, for which they gave "Crusoe" Bell a deed, and threw the remainder open for settlement.

As we are within a short run of the Samoan Islands, I may be pardoned for referring to the much-talked-of and very queer bargain and sale of that country that occurred between England and Germany. This transaction aroused considerable feeling in Australia, New Zealand and the United States, and some very pertinent questions were asked by the colonies, which brought out the following facts: Samoa lies right in the middle of the track from Australia and New Zealand to Vancouver's Island and San Francisco. Seven years ago, England, Germany and the United States made a treaty with the King of Samoa, by which they agreed to maintain him on his throne, the property of Europeans to be protected by a court consisting of the consuls of the three powers; it was further agreed that neither of the powers should annex the islands. That being the condition of things, people were much puzzled at what took place in August, 1887. King Malietoa had strictly kept all his engagements; he had ruled his people well; the islands were prospering, and a large amount of trade was being done with them, English influence being mainly predominant. In August, 1887, five German war vessels sailed into the harbor of Apia, landed six hundred armed men, and without premonition or a syllable of explanation to the English consul, carried off this native king, who was in treaty relations with England, and transported him seven thousand miles to the Cameroons, on the west coast of Africa. They then proceeded to declare the arrangement whereby three consuls had the direction of affairs at Samoa at an end, and appointed a vice-king, with a German prime minister, so that the whole direction of Samoan affairs was now in the hands of Germany, and that in face of the fact that only twelve or eighteen months ago fifty-four out of the fifty-seven native chiefs petitioned England to annex the island, on the ground that they were afraid of the Germans, and protested against German annexation. The point was that all this was done in defiance of the treaty. As far as was known, the Germans had obtained no sanction for this violation of treaty engagements, and the English consul very properly issued a protest and had it placarded, to the effect that the English government did not recognize the new king whom the Germans had set up, but would continue to recognize the king whom they had taken prisoner. Nothing happened as a result of this protest of the English consul, except that two months afterwards it was withdrawn, and the Germans were allowed to do as they pleased.

Towards the close of 1886, when England was in trouble in Egypt and their relations with some of the European powers were strained, they resigned their rights in Samoa to the German government with the understanding that they were not to be interfered with in Egypt. They did this, not only without informing the United States and the Australian colonies until months later, but absolutely without informing their own consul at Samoa. So that this unhappy man, whose duty it was to carry out the views of the English government, and who protested against what he regarded as a violation of international law, found himself in an unenviable predicament when he obtained information in September of last year, nine months "behind the fair," that the English government had agreed to the action of the Germans nine months before he received any instructions whatever. They had sacrified the natives of these islands to a rule which they detested; they had seen a king, whom they had vowed to protect, seized and transported to a distance of 7,000 miles not only without a word of protest, but with at least an implied consent, and in return they had received absolutely nothing save a promise that they should not be interfered with in Egypt, while the Egyptian campaign had gained nothing for England except the obligation of paying an enormous bill and the privilege of leaving the country at the earliest possible moment. Two months ago the Malatea party threw off the German yoke and war was commenced between them and the adherents of the vice-king and his German prime minister. Germany stands idly by and sees the poor natives kill each other.

Up to this writing they have had several bloody fights, and the end is not yet.

There is a fleet of six whaling ships cruising about in these waters, and I understand they are making money. Owing to the low price at which whale oil is now selling, no effort is made to save it. When a whale is captured the head is cut off and taken aboard, from which the bones are then taken, the body being allowed to go adrift. A good-sized head will yield about $4,000.

Speaking of heads reminds me of one I have hanging in my saloon, just opposite my berth. While in Auckland I found in a "curio shop" the head of a Mario chief who was killed in battle on the Waikato river. After much haggling, I bought it at a very high price and brought it aboard, tied a string around it and hung it from the ceiling of my room, where it bows continuously to me with every roll of the ship. When John came aboard and walked into our cabin, my chief made him a very polite bow. "Why don't you return the gentleman's courtesy?" I asked him. "What do you propose to do with that horrible thing?" John answered. "Why, take it home to my wife and babies," I replied. "Well," says John, "you will occupy this cabin alone or put that grinning skull out of sight." So, to please the old fellow I put a traveling cap on my chief's head, tied a silk scarf under his chin, and he would look very respectable if he didn't stare a fellow so completely out of countenance, and would only change the set grin he has acquired from years of solitary musing over the fat missionaries he has eaten. In a closet at the head of our bed I have a number of bows, arrows, spears and war clubs used by the Fiji Islanders and Maoris. Last night the sea became very rough, and about midnight I heard a most infernal racket going on in the closet. I called to John to know what was the matter. "You ought to know," he said; "it is that old Maori chief of yours. I saw by a flash of lightning that he had taken his head down, and now he is skirmishing around in the closet after his club, spear, etc." I jumped up and felt for my skull. It was gone. I couldn't find a match, so I commenced to feel around with my foot. Suddenly I jabbed my big toe into something that would not let go, and I commenced to yell and dance around, call for the steward and kick up Jack generally. When light was finally brought, I had dropped on the cabin floor from sheer weakness and fright, and my toe was tightly jammed in the mouth of the old cannibal chief, who, true to his hereditary instincts, was trying to make a meal of me after his long fast. This morning I secured a number of sheets of strong paper and wrapped the old savage's head up, eyes, mouth and all, and tied about 100 yards of strong twine all over him. This will keep him quiet, I hope.

The contrast between the captain and officers of the Alameda—which is the Commodore's ship—and the officers of the Mariposa, the ship we went out in, is so marked that it has been commented on in my presence on numerous occasions. Captain Morse, of the Alameda, is the jolliest, kindest-hearted gentleman I ever sailed with. His cabin is open at all times to the passengers, and any information desired is cheerfully given. No one on the ship is shown any sort of preference, and everything is done to render the long voyage pleasant. The Captain's hearty, infectious laugh can be heard at every meal, and all over the large dining saloon. On the Mariposa things were quite different. The Captain was doubtless a good officer, but I don't think the comfort or pleasure of the passengers concerned him much; as for John and myself, we had seats at his table and one of the two best staterooms on the ship, and were consequently among the favored few. We found the officers, with two exceptions, the chief engineer and chief officer Hart, a gruff lot. All seemed to be suffering from the same disease that had attacked the Captain, i. e., "the big head." An indignation meeting was talked of on account of the doctor's perfect indifference and neglect of the sick. Mr. W., quite a noted tragedian from Chicago, vowed vengeance against the M. D. for his neglect of his wife, who was suffering greatly during almost the entire trip. It is very unpleasant to have to write such disagreeable things about any one, particularly about "the bridge that has carried me safely over the dangerous chasm," yet I can truthfully say I would lay over a month rather than take this long trip by the Mariposa, and would lay over two months to go by the Alameda.

Captain Morse, of the last-named vessel, is a true, genial gentleman in the best sense of that word.

Among our passengers is Mr. Campbell, United States consul at Auckland, New Zealand. He is on his way home on leave of absence. It will be gratifying to all good Democrats to know that this is another case of Mr. Cleveland's correct judgment in putting the right man in the right place. Mr. Campbell has proved himself not only a first-class official, but a very popular gentleman with the people. We have on board a part of the London Gaiety troupe, consisting of six ladies, four gentlemen, and four servants. They did a good business in Australia, playing "Esmeralda" and "Monte Cristo." I hardly think they will do well in the United States, as it is what is known as a "leg show," and our people have about had a surfeit of shows of that character. Miss Nellie Farron and Mr. Fred. Leslie are quite clever in their way, but the jokes which our Australian cousins appreciated will scarcely be appreciated on our side of the water as being at all funny. There are two pretty good dancers in the company, Misses Linn and Grey. Judging, however, from their conversational powers, we are forced to the conclusion that they have cultivated their heels by sadly neglecting their heads. The quantities of stout champagne and other strong drink these ladies consume is something marvelous to an American.

The Oceanic Steamship Company, owned by Messrs. Spreckles & Brother, of San Francisco, consists of a fleet of four steamers of three thousand tons each. The Alameda—flag ship—Mariposa and Zealandia, run from San Francisco to Sydney, touching at Honolulu, Samoa and Auckland. The Australia plies between San Francisco and Honolulu. The sister ships Alameda and Mariposa, built by Clapp of Philadelphia, cost $500,000 each; the Zealandia and Australia, cost $250,000 each. They were bought from an opposition line. The cost, per ship, of a round trip to Sydney and return, is $50,000 Each ship makes four trips a year. We will estimate the passenger receipts at $20,000, and freight at $20,000 per round trip, i. e., San Francisco to Sydney and back to " Frisco," in all three months. They are paid a subsidy by New South Wales and New Zealand of £32,-000, or $150,000, and are allowed all the postage by our government on mail matter carried by them, which amounts to about $50,000 per year. The life of an ocean steamer is from ten to fifteen years. Taking this into consideration, together with the original cost of the " plant," Messrs. Spreckels haven't a very paying investment in this line.

First-class passage from " Frisco" to Sydney is $200; steerage, $100. The Alameda and Mariposa are by far the best for first class passengers, while the Zealandia and Australia are much the best for steerage, as they were originally fitted for only first-class and second-class, and the steerage now occupies the second-class accommodations.

www.ingramcontent.com/pod-product-compliance
Lightning Source LLC
Chambersburg PA
CBHW020127170426
43199CB00009B/666